# LANGUAGE TEACHING GAMES AND CONTESTS
## Second revised edition

# LANGUAGE TEACHING GAMES AND CONTESTS

## Second revised edition

**W R LEE**

**Oxford University Press**

*Oxford University Press, Walton Street, Oxford OX2 6DP*

OXFORD
NEW YORK TORONTO MELBOURNE AUCKLAND
PETALING JAYA SINGAPORE HONG KONG TOKYO
DELHI BOMBAY CALCUTTA MADRAS KARACHI
NAIROBI DAR ES SALAAM CAPE TOWN

and associated companies in
BERLIN IBADAN

OXFORD, OXFORD ENGLISH, and the
OXFORD ENGLISH logo are trade marks of
Oxford University Press

ISBN 0 19 432716 7

© W. R. Lee 1979

First published 1979
Second revised edition 1986
Fourth impression 1990

Cover illustration by John Montgomery

Printed in Hong Kong

# 17974539

*To all teachers who*
*believe that in*
*foreign language teaching*
*enjoyment and success*
*go together*

# CONTENTS

# ACKNOWLEDGEMENTS

The author is grateful to many people, and not least to his former students at the University of London Institute of Education, and to the teachers and children he has taught or worked with on language teachers' courses in many countries of the world. He still records with pleasure a debt to those who contributed ideas to the first edition, but since that time this debt has so greatly increased that it would now hardly be possible to mention names. Some idea of its extent will be gained from the bibliography, itself an abbreviated one, and from frequent footnotes in which specific acknowledgements are made. He would like in particular to thank Cristina Whitecross and others at Oxford University Press for their painstaking and constructive criticisms and much heavy work on the untidy detail of the new text.

# INTRODUCTION

It is now very generally accepted that language teaching not merely can be but should be enjoyable. This is not to assume that it is easy, but only that there is no need, by excluding enjoyment, to make it more difficult.

Games are enjoyable. The essence of many games lies in outstripping, in friendly fashion, someone else's performance, or (and adult learners often prefer this) in bettering one's own, as in the world of sport. The goal is visible and stimulating: outdoing others, and improving on oneself, are by and large enjoyable pursuits. Enjoyable also is the active co-operation with one's fellows. In group or team activity, rivalry and co-operation go hand in hand. There are the other groups or teams to surpass, and friends to help surpass them. One's own activity takes on importance in the latter's eyes. But in spite of all the effort – and sometimes, when attention is sharply focused and the learner's energies stretched to the full in a game, it is hard to see any difference between 'work' and 'play' – there is a pleasant, informal, and often relaxed atmosphere, favourable to language learning.

Nevertheless, the case for language games is not identical with the case for enjoyment in the language lesson. An agreeable although busy atmosphere can be attained by other means, even if games are absent, and games have other and equally important virtues. They banish boredom and so make for willing learners, who look forward to language lessons. But after all, any kind of interesting activity would make them do that. We should ask, therefore, what other advantage language learning games offer than the creation of an enjoyable atmosphere in which to learn.

A language is learnt by using it – and this means using it in situations and communicatively. Disembodied sounds, words, phrases, and sentences, however wrapped about with rules, do not carry language learning far; although it is helpful up to a point to remove such elements and look at them closely, much as

1

one examines components of a machine, before returning them to the intermingling streams of discourse.

The situations which bring a foreign language to life in the classroom are provided by gestures, by handling and touching things, by incidents and activities, by pictures, by dramatization, by interesting stories spoken or in print – and not least by certain contests and games. In these the language is linked with action and is no longer a disembodied thing.

The majority of the games described in this book give the learners experience of communicating with the help of the foreign language: one might indeed call them 'communication games'. It is through experience of communication in the language they are learning that language learners best learn how to communicate in it.

'Communication games' are not necessarily lengthy or complex. There is something to be communicated to others or to be found out from others, and the learners want to keep the game going because they are interested in it. Moreover, unless they succeed in communicating the game falls flat and comes to an end. This is true of such a game as *Number Change*, at first sight apparently 'non-communicative'; but unless those who speak are understood by those who hear, the game goes wrong and the learners are not satisfied. Some of the vocabulary games are rather different: in adding extra words the learners are demonstrating their own knowledge, but to fellow learners. There is a communicative aspect to this activity too; the knowledge is shared.

Although it is extremely doubtful (and the present author does not believe) that *all* language games, still less all forms of language learning activity, must be 'communicative' in order to aid language learning, there are few games in this book that have no communicative aspect, and most provide the learners with communicative experience of one sort and another from beginning to end: sometimes the communication is partly linguistic and partly non-linguistic, sometimes one group or one person knows something another does not (as in the guessing games), sometimes neither knows, and often there is an interesting fiction (in *Alibi* nobody has committed a burglary, for instance). Language subserves different modes and degrees of communication, and language games are equally varied.

Most language games distract the learners' attention from the study of linguistic forms. They stop thinking *about* the language and instead *use* it, receptively or productively, as a means of considering something else, as those with an advanced command of the language use it too.

Repetition is basic to language learning, but not the repetition of mechanical drills, although in the writer's view they should not be entirely eliminated. But it seems to be repetition of *successful and interesting* communication which counts and which has the most encouraging, 'language advancing', and motivating effect. This kind of repetition is found in many language games. There can be *un*interesting communication too, which does nothing to sustain motivation.

Games, therefore, should not be regarded as a marginal activity, filling in odd moments when the teacher and class have nothing better to do. Certainly there are such games, a few of which are included in this book, and there are end-of-term and party games, which are given a section, but on the whole the games here described should be central to the language teaching programme. A game may of course be excellent as a game and yet of no value as an aid to language learning. Although the word *game* has been taken in a broad sense, such games are not included. Games in the strict sense, which have a definite beginning and end and are governed by rules, shade off into game-like activities which have a less formal design. There is no clear-cut line of division in language teaching between games and non-games.

Language learning itself is complex and many-sided, which need not discourage us from seeing it crudely as a matter of four communicative skills: listening, reading, speaking, and writing. Success here is to be judged by the degree to which the language user can grasp the meaning of what is said or printed, or convey the meaning of what he writes or says. There are games in this book to develop all these skills.

A grouping into games for young children, for older children, and for adults was rejected because, although the book includes games for all three, it is often very much a matter of opinion and local circumstance to which of these categories a particular game belongs. The author's experience is that there are numerous children's games which adults like playing, particularly if they see the language learning point.

3

There are games here too, for various stages of achievement, from very elementary to advanced, as well as games for classes, teams, and groups, games requiring simple or no apparatus, and outdoor and indoor games. Group activity and pair activity are of special importance in playing some of the games, and in increasing the extent to which the learners are actively involved. Finally, there are games which give practice in the use of particular language patterns.

## Organization of the class

Many of these games depend for their success, like other teaching, on good class organization. Forethought is indispensable.

Division into teams or groups, for instance, should not have to be done afresh on every occasion: this is a waste of time. On the whole it is best for a learner, especially for a child, to be in the same team throughout the year, and it disturbs a child's sense of 'belonging' to be switched arbitrarily from one team to another. If for some reason, perhaps because of absences, a team or group falls below strength, allowance can be made when there is point-scoring.

If teams or groups are to be named, the names should be suitable. *Sparrows*, *Robins*, and *Skylarks* may please young children (in countries where these birds are known of), while older children may look upon such labels with scorn. *Lions* and *Tigers* have a broader appeal; colours and cardinal points are still more widely acceptable. Much depends on the country you are teaching in and on the learners' ages. As it is impossible to find team names which are universally suitable, 'A', 'B', etc. have been used in this book, and it is up to teacher and class to breathe life into these letters in their own way.

If there is to be any sort of competition or contest between teams, they should be evenly matched. When the more advanced or more backward learners are unevenly distributed, certain groups or teams always win and this is discouraging for the others.

Teams are larger than groups. In a class of average size (say, 30) with two teams, there could easily be three groups in each team. Organization into groups, all of which can be active at the same time, is one way of multiplying language practice. Four or five in a group are enough. The teacher should be able to get from group

4

to group quickly, and this may mean that furniture has to be rearranged. If the classroom is unbearably crowded, it may be possible, depending on the climate and weather, to leave it. At some schools the writer has seen good lessons taking place under the trees outside.

Pair activity (work in twos) can give a still greater amount of communicative practice, though there is less opportunity for consultation and mutual correction. Many of the games in this book call for, or at least allow for, activity in pairs.

Useful though pair activity and group activity are, however, we have to be content with teams where the classroom is very crowded and there is nowhere else to go. How many teams should there be? Two may be enough and is a very manageable number – perhaps the left-hand and right-hand halves of the class. Three is a reasonable number too – the middle and the two sides. Or the teams may be split. Thus in a class of thirty-six (a below average size in many countries) sitting in six rows of single desks, there could be the following arrangement for two teams (A and B):

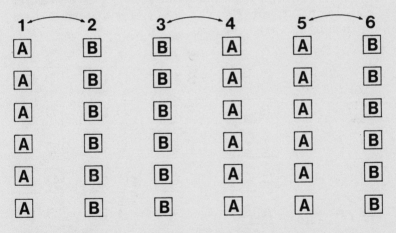

For pair activity, members of the class face their opposite number by turning sideways, and desks can be pushed towards or against each other if necessary. If for some reason the members of the teams need to be all together, only the two outside lines (1 and 6) need change seats.

A class of the same size could have three teams (A, B, and C) seated thus:

|  | 1 | 2 | 3 | 4 | 5 | 6 |
|---|---|---|---|---|---|---|
|  | A | B | C | A | B | C |
|  | A | B | C | A | B | C |
|  | A | B | C | A | B | C |
|  | A | B | C | A | B | C |
|  | A | B | C | A | B | C |
|  | A | B | C | A | B | C |

For each of the three teams to form a block, lines 2 and 4 and also 3 and 5 would have to change places.

With a big class it may be livelier to have four teams. Here is a possible seating plan for a class of 48 pupils seated in twos (i.e. at double desks). The plan allows of easy work in pairs between members of the same team, and the lines are easily switched over (e.g. 2 with 3, 6 with 7, 8 with 9) to ensure that members of different teams are neighbours.

|  | 1 2 | 3 4 | 5 6 | 7 8 | 9 10 |
|---|---|---|---|---|---|
| 1 | A A | B B | B B | C C | D D |
| 2 | A A | B B | B B | C C | D D |
| 3 | A A | B B | B B | C C | D D |
| 4 | A A | C C | C C | C C | D D |
| 5 | A A | A A | - - | D D | D D |

People cannot learn a language really well and enjoyably unless from time to time they can move about and do things while speaking it, and it is therefore a great advantage if they can get out readily from their seats.

Unless the classroom is small, it is unwise to have any team (or any learners) permanently at the back, where it may be harder to hear.

Here is a plan for two teams in a class of 25, by which activity with a learner belonging to the other team can be obtained both in front (or behind) and at the side, members of different teams being seated alternately.

| 1 | 2 | 3 | 4 | 5 |
|---|---|---|---|---|
| A | B | A | B | A |
| B | A | B | A | B |
| A | B | A | B | A |
| B | A | B | A | B |
| A | B | A | B | A |

In a children's class teams may be distinguished by team badges or colours.

Classrooms nowadays, especially those for young children, are often equipped with light and easily moved tables, around each of which a group of learners may sit. It is an advantage for older learners, too, to have plenty of space and to be able to move easily about the room. Various arrangements of furniture are desirable for various activities. Sometimes the furniture gets in the way and it is necessary to push it back against the walls, e.g. for dramatization. It is a pity if the class and teacher are at the mercy of fixed benches or desks: it is a great help if arrangements are flexible. This is true for adults also.

Children should not normally be separated from their friends.

## Scoring

When points are scored, it is advisable to vary the method of scoring. Psychologically it is better to give points for success than to take them away for failure, even if this procedure keeps the scorers very busy.

Images of things which climb or expand are useful as means of visually representing the score. Thus if the number of points likely to be scored is small, they can be marked on ladders as they are won. The scores of four teams might look something like this:

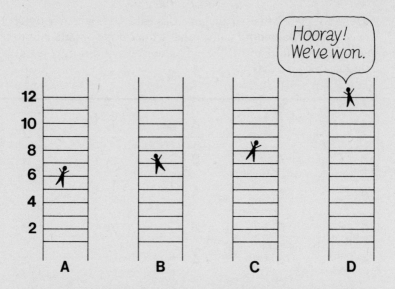

Human or animal shapes (e.g. stick figures) interest children more than mere dots or abstract symbols, and with coloured chalks each can be different. Where blackboard space is limited, one ladder can show several scores. If 'long-term' team scores are to be shown (e.g. weekly or monthly totals), more substantial ladders, on the rungs of which cardboard figures can be hooked, may be worth making. When there is a maximum possible score the ladders can have an appropriate number of rungs leading up to a definite goal, such as the roof of a house or the top of a tower. For some games (e.g. 'Word-guessing') each team's score can be shown on a flight of steps, thus:

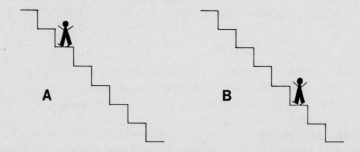

For each letter correctly guessed, the team figure moves one step up, for each incorrect letter one step down.

Another way of showing scores as they increase is to sketch one symbol for each point along a horizontal line: simple trees, fish, fruit, windmills, tents, ducks, faces (the expressions getting more cheerful as the line lengthens) – any symbol that can be drawn very quickly and simply and that has a certain appeal to the learner. The objects may of course be associated with the names of the teams, especially if these are animal, bird, or flower names. Here are some examples.

3 pts

3 pts

2 pts

6 pts

There are lots of visual possibilities of this sort: adding waggons to a train, sleepers to a railway track, stars to a sky, branches to a tree, bricks to a wall, etc. The teacher's imagination and ingenuity should get to work, starting always from knowledge of the learners. Anything that makes the learning go with an extra swing is worthwhile.

Scores can also be registered non-visually: stones or marbles or peas can be dropped into bags, nuts or beads or beans placed in bowls, sticks laid in bundles. These are countable things, like the less interesting ticks or crosses or numbers on the blackboard. At a given moment, nevertheless, the score is unknown: it has to be reckoned up subsequently. Visual representation, on the other hand, runs along side by side with the game.

Scoring in games which merely have winners can be shown as above or more simply. A house or tower can be built up on the board stone by stone, one stone for every point, and the winner has the biggest or tallest building. Boats may cross a lake or sea inch by inch, the winner being the first to reach the other side.

It is a mistake to think that adults (i.e. the over-fifteens) are not interested in the competitive element in certain games. Frequently it is obvious that it is this most of all that stimulates them to make a special effort. They are interested also, where there is scoring, in seeing it registered.

These are examples only, and the inventive teacher will be able to choose and adapt. It is easy to overdo competition, of course, and point-scoring is not needed every day. Procedures must be varied. It is essential, however, that lessons should be well prepared and pleasantly and brightly conducted, so that learners actively use the language most of the time.

## Learner participation

As with other language learning activities, one of the problems about games is to get everybody to take a full part. What ways are there of ensuring that the shyer or less advanced learners also take part actively? Here are a few suggestions, not all of which may need to be or even can be adopted in every instance.

(i) Sometimes a few minutes' silent preparation – time to think, and perhaps even to make a note or two – will help an oral game (e.g. a guessing game) to go more quickly.

(ii) Often, it will help to put 'reminder' words or phrases on the board, e.g. question beginnings (*Do*, *When*, *Where*, etc.) and vocabulary the class knows. At any stage in an elementary course, the teacher should know what words and phrases the learners can already use to communicate in the language, and what they are still uncertain of. With a slow class the 'reminder' material could include whole sentences (of a type suitable to the game) displayed in the form of a substitution table. e.g. for one type of guessing game:

| | | | | |
|---|---|---|---|---|
| | in | the | bag | |
| | on | a | pocket | |
| | under | that | box | |
| Is it | behind | those | cupboard | ? |
| | on top of | his | book [s] | |
| | among | her | pencil [s] | |
| | | your | flower [s] | |
| | | —'s | foot | |

etc

Guesses can be but need not be read from such a table, with the help of which nobody need be silent. It can be added to, especially in the last column, if guesses begin to dry up.

(iii)   Let one of the learners, or several in turn, lead the activity while you yourself sit in the class and take part. You can whisper suggestions to those who do not know what to say, or you can write down a word or two on a slip of paper and pass it to them to give them an idea. Sit near those who most require help.

(iv)   If you are asking for 'Hands up', take care not to call upon the same people over and over again to respond. Distribute your attention over the whole class. Give hints to help shy or slow learners to speak.

(v)   Consider whether the game – possibly after the class as a whole has played it – can also be played in groups or pairs. If it can, this in itself increases the amount of participation. Use group and pair activity as much as possible.

(vi)   Mutual help within the class, or within the team or group, should be encouraged. Often it is possible, in these games, to have questions, etc, put to one team or group by members of other teams or groups, who can prepare in collaboration what they need to say, so that everyone has something to offer.

Relatively few games in this book call for preliminary explanation which cannot be given, with the aid of prompting and gesture, in the foreign language itself. This, after all, is in itself a valuable exercise in communication. Many of them do not require explanation so much as practical demonstration of how they should be played, and the teacher has first to join in the game, acting as a leader. Then, if there is a leading role, others can take it in turn.

Language games are sometimes played at a language level below that reached by the learners, and thus the game is insufficiently demanding and does not stretch the learners' command.

Some of the games contained in this book are familiar, for many sources have been consulted, and others have been invented by the author. Nearly all the games have been tried out at one time or another with classes, by the author, his students, or other teachers. Nevertheless, in some circumstances they will need adaptation: not all are suitable everywhere, regardless of the kind of classroom or class.

11

One more introductory point – games bring teacher and learners into a more agreeable and more intimate relationship, and that too helps to ease the process of learning and teaching.

*Note.* For the present revised and considerably expanded edition a new division into chapters has been adopted and the text extensively rewritten and in places shortened. In addition, presentation of the games has been simplified. Most chapter headings are self-explanatory but what the reader needs may also be sought in the indexes, which are fuller than in the original edition. Many new games or variants of games have been added.

*Playing-time:* most games take from five to ten minutes. If more time is needed, this will be stated.

# Chapter 1
# STRUCTURE GAMES

*Many games provide experience of the use of particular patterns of syntax in communication, and these are here called structure games. Among them are a number of guessing games which can be played at various age levels. In general, the challenge to guess arouses considerable interest and encourages the learners to communicate what they see as possible 'right answers'.*

## 1 What is it? Is it...?

|  |  |
|---|---|
| Level | **elementary, intermediate, and advanced** |
| Age | **any** |
| Group size | **whole class, groups, or pairs** |
| Use | **to practise 'yes-no' and other questions and to brush up vocabulary** |

Somebody thinks of an object or person the class knows the name of, and the others ask questions, putting up their hands and waiting to be called on: *Is it a green book? Is it Mary's desk? Is it my face? Is it the door? Is it John and Peter? Is it the railway station? Is it the man who came here this morning?* etc. The first to guess correctly takes the 'thinker's' place.

After such a game has been successfully played by the class as a whole, it can be played in groups or even in pairs.

The learner who has thought of something may be questioned by members of another team only, and points scored according to the number of questions asked (e.g. one point for a guess after only five questions). There should be a frequent change from one team to another, to keep the whole class active.

The number of *yes-no* questions may be limited (e.g. to twenty), after which the answer must be given and the game started again.

## Variants

*A*   Except perhaps at a very elementary level, when learners do not know many words, the 'field' may be circumscribed, so that particular vocabulary is brought into play (e.g. *I'm thinking of something in the room/in the school/at the seaside/on the farm/at home*, etc.). At a rather more advanced stage the guessing may take some such form as *She's thinking about the time when she . . .* , *They're thinking about how they . . .* , *You're thinking about the day you . . .* , etc.

*B*   One learner from each of two teams goes outside. These two decide on an object or person, return to the room, and join *opposite* teams, by whom they are asked questions (which could be restricted to *yes-no* questions). The first team to find out the answer is the winner.

*C*   Two go out. The class chooses an object or person in the classroom or visible in a picture. The two come back and alternately ask questions such as *Is it Mary's bag? Is it that picture? Is it the ink-mark on George's nose? Is it his desk?* (pointing), etc.

*D*   Learners in turn think of an object and others ask them questions beginning with *how, when, where,* or *which.* Thus: *Where it is kept? How do you hold it? When do you need it?* Questions beginning with *where* and *why* may also be appropriate. Some of the questions may be unanswered.

*E*   There is an unknown object in a box, which can be tilted, gently shaken, smelt, listened to, etc. but not opened. Questions such as *What can you hear? What's it made of? Is it heavy or light? Can you smell anything? What sort of sound/smell is it?* , etc. can be asked. Teach the students to ask such questions also: do not do all the talking yourself. After a minute or two, the learners write down what they think the object is, and add why (i.e. they describe the 'clues'). Alternatively they write *I don't know what it is, but it sounds like . . .* , etc. Possible objects: a nail, two nails, buttons, ping-pong balls, a tennis ball, a small sponge, a large stone and two small ones, a pack of cards, milk-bottle tops, coins (how many?), coffee beans, tea leaves, a glass paper-weight, nuts, a knife and fork, a potato, rice, a key (what kind?), some sand, a baby's rattle, etc.

*F*   Any small objects of which the names are known are put on a tray and covered by a newspaper or cloth. Members of different teams come out, feel them, and answer the question *What is it?* This sounds easy, but is not if the objects are wrapped. Each one has a guess. The first to guess right scores a team point.

G Several learners face the class with hands behind their backs. Somebody puts small wrapped objects (e.g. a rubber, a nut, sweets, coffee beans, a marble, a lump of sugar, a candle, a key, buttons) into their hands, and each has to feel and guess what they are. As soon as all have guessed, they unwrap their objects in turn and show them. *Were you right, X? Was he/she right?* Collective answers can be given.

H *Mystery drawings.* The teacher gives the idea of this game by drawing a few objects simply on the board (e.g. a ship, a house, a car, a pram, an aeroplane), asking as he goes along *What's this?* or perhaps, at a slightly more advanced level, *What's this going to be?* Then he rubs out some of the essential lines and says about one of the drawings, as if puzzled, *Now what was this? Oh yes, I know, it was a . . .* He does the same with a second drawing, and then asks the class about the others. *And what's this?* They say *It's a pram/an aeroplane*, etc. He then draws the first line of something new and again asks. The pupils guess *It's an umbrella/a bicycle/a spider/an elephant*, etc. One or two lines are added to help the guesses along, and when the right guess is made the remaining lines are drawn in. Pupils can also 'be the teacher' and make such drawings on the board themselves.

## 2 Who am I? What's my name?

| | |
|---|---|
| Level | **intermediate** |
| Age | **any (except young children). Variants D, E, & F: young children** |
| Group size | **whole class, groups, pairs (not for all variants)** |
| Use | **to practise 'yes-no' questions and to brush up vocabulary** |

Everybody imagines himself to be somebody else – a living person well-known locally, nationally, or internationally, or an historical figure such as Napoleon, Gandhi, Julius Caesar, Queen Elizabeth I, Shakespeare, Isaac Newton, Galileo, or Homer. Each makes up two short sentences about himself or herself, e.g. *I lived in . . . about . . . years ago. I was a king/ queen/poet/general/scientist*, etc. There is usually not much difficulty in guessing, but it should not be made too easy (e.g. one should not say, if one is Shakespeare, *I lived in Stratford-on-Avon and wrote Hamlet!*).

## Variants

*A*  This game can of course be played in the third person as *What is he/she?* or *What are they?* The questions are then put indirectly, that is, one member of the class asks another to find out, e.g. *Ask him whether he lives in this country. Do you live in this country? Ask him whether he's a well-known tennis-player. Are you a well-known tennis-player?*, etc. Responses: *Yes, I am.* (*He says he is.*), etc. *No, I'm not* (*He says he isn't.*), etc. Plurals can also be used. *What are we?* (*Ask them whether . . .*). *They say they . . .*), etc.

*B*  Each learner decides who he or she is and is questioned by others.

*C*  Everybody has a name and/or an occupation on a piece of paper pinned to his or her back, and has to ask others questions in order to discover what the name and occupation are. Possible questions: *Do I work out of doors? Do I have to get up early in the morning? Do I stay in the same place all the time?*

*D*  *Voices.* One child stands near the wall and faces it, not too near the others. Various children say in turn, disguising their voices, *Good morning* (or *Good afternoon*), . . . The child at the wall replies, if he thinks he recognises the voice, *Good morning* (or *Good afternoon*), . . . If he cannot guess, or guesses wrongly, he changes place with the speaker.

The wording may be varied. For instance, the child at the wall may ask *Is that . . . ?* or *I think that's . . .*

*E*  *Queenie.* One girl stands with her back to the others and throws a ball over her head. One of the children picks it up and they all chant, standing in line:

> *Queenie, Queenie,*
> *Who's got the ball?*
> *Is she big or is she small,*
> *Is she fat or is she thin,*
> *Or is she like a rolling-pin?*

*Queenie* then guesses who has the ball. She may turn round to do so if the others have their hands behind their backs. If she is right she stays where she is; otherwise, she changes places with the one who has the ball[1].

F   The children pretend to be animals and the others guess by asking questions such as *Are you big or small? Where do you live? What do you eat? What colour are you?* etc. (Small children.)

# 3  What is there in my bag today?

Level   **elementary and intermediate**
Age   **children**
Group size   **whole class, groups, and pairs**
Use   **to brush up vocabulary and to practise 'there's', 'there are' (or 'have you', 'have you got')**

Alternatively: *What's in my bag today? What have I got in my bag today?* (This can be the teacher's or anybody's bag, no doubt specially prepared.)

The children guess, for instance, *There's an apple/a photograph/a mirror/a handkerchief/a season ticket/a doll/a sandwich*, etc. and the owner of the bag says *No, there isn't a . . .* or *Yes, there's a . . .* and brings it out and perhaps asks *What colour is it?* or *Is it a big . . . or a small . . . ?* At an appropriate level plurals come in naturally here, e.g. *There are some postcards/sweets/letters/coins in my bag.*

There could also be pictures and models in the bag, to make the game more interesting. *There's a big plane, there's a green car, there are some trees, there's a man with a funny hat*, etc. Models and pictures should be large enough for everyone to see.

## Variants

A   Two learners (say, Anne and George) each have a bag containing objects (or pictures or models of objects). Learners take turns, the teams alternating, to guess what there is in the bags. Guesses (in the form of statements or questions) are directed at Anne by members of the team George belongs to (Team G), and at George by members of the team Anne belongs to (Team A). For example:
Anne: *There's a small bottle in your bag, George.*
George: *No, there isn't a small bottle.*
But if there is a small bottle in Anne's bag, she says so:

Anne: *But there* is *a small bottle in mine*, and her team (A) scores a point.
George: *There's a horse in your bag, Anne* (or a picture of a horse).
Anne: *No, there isn't.*
George keeps quiet, because he hasn't got a horse either. No point scored by either team.
Anne: *There's a piano in your bag, George.*
George: *Yes, there is. There's a piano.* He shows the picture and puts it down on the table. One point for Team A.

The objects included should reflect the learners' interests at their age of learning, but can also be an aid to the brushing up of vocabulary.

There can be renaming of the objects as they are put back in the bags afterwards.

B   The learners work in pairs and take turns to guess the contents of each other's bags.

There are various linguistic possibilities, *Is there a . . . ? There's a . . ., Are there any . . . ? There are some . . . , There's a . . ., isn't there? There are some . . . , aren't there?* etc.

# 4   Where is it?

| | |
|---|---|
| Level | **elementary and intermediate** |
| Age | **any** |
| Group size | **whole class** |
| Use | **to practise prepositional phrases. (Variant B: also the 'may' of possibility.)** |

Learners turn round and close their eyes while a small object (or several objects) such as a coin, a ring, a sweet, or a small doll is hidden. Questions: *Is it behind the cupboard/in X's pocket/in Y's desk/in your shoe/under those books?* etc. Each learner should make at least one guess. Statements can be made instead of questions: *It's behind the cupboard/in X's pocket*, etc.

## Variants

A   Using tag-questions: *It's behind the cupboard, isn't it?* etc.
B   A small object is hidden. Where can it possibly be? Everybody suggests a place: *It may be in your pocket/on top of the*

*cupboard/in Tom's desk/behind that picture/in the waste-paper-basket*, etc. A team point for the first to guess correctly, using *may*. *Might* or *could* are also possible. *It might/could be in your pocket. Could it be in your pocket?*

C Using the past: *I've just found this button*, etc. *Guess where it was. It was behind the cupboard/in the drawer of your table/under the vase*, etc. *No, it wasn't there* or *Yes, that's right*.

D Several learners go out of the room while a small object is hidden. They know what the object is. On re-entering the room, each in turn asks a question, naming someone to answer it. This is done three times. Thus if there are six questioners, eighteen different learners are asked a question. The six in front listen carefully to each other's questions, which they may have planned together before they came in, and especially to the answers. They try to guess where the object is before they finish asking all their questions.

Only *yes-no* questions are permitted, e.g. *Is it on anybody's finger? Is it on the floor? Is it near us? Is it in the teacher's pocket? It's in your desk, Peter, isn't it?* and so on.

As soon as a successful guess is made, another group (which should include learners who have not had a chance of speaking) goes outside and another object is hidden.

E Hide a puppet, or a cut-out of an animal (e.g. a cat), before the lesson. Say *I've lost . . .* (naming the puppet), or *I've lost my cat. Where is he?* The learners guess. *He's in your bag outside the room/behind those big books*, etc. (For young children.)

## 5  Out of place

|  |  |
|---|---|
| Level | **intermediate** |
| Age | **any** |
| Group size | **whole class** |
| Use | **to practise 'there's' and prepositional phrases, the present perfect (Variants A and B), the passive (B), and 'should/shouldn't', 'ought'/'oughtn't'** |

At least a dozen objects are placed beforehand in unfamiliar positions, all being in 'full' view. The learners are not told what the objects are, but are given a minute or two to look about them, and then are asked to say what they have noticed. They may say, for instance: *There's a book on top of the door. There's a bag in the waste-paper-basket. There's a hairbrush on the record-player. There's a ruler in the vase*, etc.

At another stage the past tense could be used, if the objects have been taken away. Thus: *There was a book on top of the door. Was there? Yes, there was. Is there a book there now? No, there isn't.*

Or, if some of the objects have been removed and not others, one of the uses of *still* can be practised. *Is it still there? No. Is my bag still there? Yes, it is – it's still in the corner.*

## Variants

A *Changes*. Somebody goes outside to do something, and the result must be fairly visible, but preferably not too obvious, when he or she returns. *What has he/she done? He/She has combed his hair/done up her shoelaces/taken off his pullover/undone the second button of his jacket*, etc. A point for any prompt and correct answer.

B *What has been done?* Everybody takes a quick look round the classroom, noticing where various objects are. One group goes outside and certain objects are quickly moved. The group outside returns and each member of it says what has happened, e.g. *The table has been turned round. The flowers have been taken away. The blackboard has been moved to the other side of the table. Paul and John have changed places. Lola has taken off her ring. The two pictures have been changed over*, etc. If it is not clear who has made the change, the passive will be used.

C As with B except that the learners say: *It shouldn't be . . .* (wherever it is): *it should be . . .* (somewhere else); alternatively: *ought to.*

D The learners can be asked to write down what they have noticed before anybody says anything. Points may be scored for correct observation.

# 6 Finding the objects

Level **elementary and intermediate**
Age **children**
Group size **whole class (small)**
Use **to practise one use of 'the', prepositions of place, and reading and writing**

A number of small objects, of which each player has a list, have been hidden about the room, and a limited time is allowed for finding them. As each player finds an object, he or she goes somewhere nearby and writes down what and where it is, e.g. *The key is behind a book in the cupboard. The teaspoon is under the vase of flowers. The ball of wool is in the box on the window-ledge,* etc. The first to find all the objects and write down sentences about them is the winner, but the sentences should be evaluated too. (The form of the sentence can be prescribed, e.g. as *The ... is...* or *I have found the ...* but not *There's a ...* , since particular objects mentioned on the list are being looked for and the definite article is therefore required.)

The more hiding-places there are in the room the better.

## Variants

*A* The children do not leave their places. They close their eyes while a fairly small object (e.g. a coloured ball, a banana, a doll, a sock) is placed somewhere in the room where it is not entirely hidden. An 'observer' from each team can be appointed to see that the eyes of the other team are all kept shut. Further, there should be misleading movements about the room while the object is being placed. *Now open your eyes. Don't say anything. I've hidden a bag of sweets* (or whatever). *Fold your arms when you see where it is.* As soon as several in each team have done this, ask the class, or individuals: *Where's the bag of sweets? (It's on the cupboard/on your chair/in that box,* etc.).

*B* Small objects are half-hidden. The children (in a small class) are free to move about in order to see where they are, but there is no need to move anything. When they have located the object or objects, they return to their seats. Then the teacher or a pupil asks the class: *Where's the tennis-ball?* etc. and the answer is given.

C Numerous objects are hidden and each team or group leader has a list (in words or pictures). The leaders stay where they are, while the others search. When an object is found it is not moved and nothing is said to the other searchers: the finder swiftly goes to the team or group leader, who ticks it off on the list. The first team or group to have all the objects ticked off is the winner.[2]

# 7 Where am I/are we/is he? etc.

|  |  |
|---|---|
| Level | **elementary and intermediate** |
| Age | **children** |
| Group size | **whole class or groups** |
| Use | **to practise 'yes-no' questions and to brush up vocabulary** |

In imagination you can be almost anywhere, but there can be some limit, e.g. you have to be somewhere in the school, in the town, or in the big picture (perhaps a street scene or a picture of a railway station or even of the inside of a house) hanging on the wall. So you are not always free to be 'on the moon': the situation can be restricted.

Briefly explain the idea of the game and then let everybody guess where you, the teacher, are. Shut your eyes for a moment as if to imagine it. *Are you on a bus going to . . . ? (No, I'm not.) Are you on the beach? (No, I'm not on the beach.) Are you at home, looking at TV? (No.) Are you asleep in bed? (No, I'm awake.) Are you sailing a boat on the river?* And so on.

Of course, the game may be more fun if no limit is placed on the possibilities. This will appeal to boys and girls: *Are you fighting a lion in Africa? Are you rowing a boat across the Atlantic?* but will tend to go on much too long before the right guess is made. You can cut the guessing short by giving hints.

Each may write down on a piece of paper where he or she is supposed to be, and show it to you before the questions begin.

Two or three learners may decide jointly where they are, responding to the suggestions in turn (*We . . .*). There may also be an 'indirect' approach: *Is he . . . Are they . . . ? I'll ask him/them. Are you . . . ? No, I'm not/we're not. He/They say(s) he/they aren't.* The teacher should work the procedure out carefully beforehand.

## Variants

*A* Using the past tense or present perfect tense. *Where was I yesterday? Where have I been this afternoon?* Similar imaginary places can be mentioned, or real places especially after a holiday break.

*B* Each learner or group describes a scene (fairly familiar to everybody in the class) mentioning only what can be seen, heard, smelt, or touched when they are there, but not giving a name to the place. Others take turns to guess.

This can be done orally or in writing. If the descriptions are written, they are read aloud.

# 8 Whose is it?

| | |
|---|---|
| Level | **elementary** |
| Age | **children** |
| Group size | **whole class** |
| Use | **to practise possessive pronouns** |

Objects belonging to various learners are placed beforehand in various parts of the room. They are all visible. For example, there could be a red pencil on one of the desks (all other pens and pencils should be put away), a black raincoat hanging at the side of the blackboard, a pencil-box on a chair, a pair of shoes near the door, an apple or an orange on a shelf, etc. The objects should be numerous and *they should not be familiar*, e.g. the coat should not be one which a particular pupil in the class always wears.

The game proceeds as follows. Hold up or point to one of the objects and ask *What's this?* or *What are these? A pair of shoes.* Then talk about them a bit, e.g. *Are they black or brown? Are they girls' shoes or boys' shoes?* Then ask *Whose are they?* or *Who do they belong to?* and guesses are made. *They're Mary's.* Mary says: *No, they aren't mine. They're Alison's. Are they yours, Alison? No. No, they aren't hers.* And so on, until the right guess is made. The guesses may of course be either statements or questions.

If there are many objects of a kind, e.g. many books, scarves, coats, or oranges, *which* and pronominal *one* will also be needed. *Which coat is yours/his?* etc. (pointing) *Which book is Eve's? The one on the table? Or that long one?* etc.

The materials needed for this game are many common objects which belong to the learners, but which they do not normally have at school.

## 9 Lucky dip

| | |
|---|---|
| Level | **fairly elementary** |
| Age | **young children** |
| Group size | **whole class (small)** |
| Use | **to practise possessives and to brush up vocabulary** |

This is an occasional activity for a small class. The children, and also the teacher, put various articles (including models) into a large bag. Later, everybody takes out one without looking to see what it is. Informal conversation: *What have you got, Pamela? An aeroplane, miss. Oh, that's good. What have you got, Jack? What's it called? A calendar.* And so on.

If most of the articles belong to the children, there can now be exchange. *Whose is this? Is this yours or his? It's mine*, etc.

A few of the articles, not belonging to the children, can be marked 'First prize', 'Second prize', etc. These will be kept by those who have them.

There may also be a few 'messages' inside small envelopes, e.g. *Find something behind this cupboard. Look in my left pocket. There is something behind the green books.* The articles hidden there should be similar to those in the bag.

Everybody gets his own article back, and may get another one also.

Teach the children to ask *one another* some of the questions, so that the teacher is not the only one to talk.

## 10 Getting your things back

Level **elementary and intermediate**
Age **any**
Group size **whole class**
Use **to practise possessive pronouns**

Various objects belonging to members of the class are collected together and put in a bag. Later, somebody takes them out one at a time, asking such questions as *Whose is this? Is this Hilary's? Is this watch yours, John? Whose . . . is this?* Answers: *It's mine. It's Peter's. It's his* (pointing to him) etc. If some of the teacher's belongings are there too: *It's Mr/Mrs/Miss X's.*

### Variants

*A* As the objects are taken out, those they belong to stand up and say *That's mine. That's my diary*, etc. and so get them back, provided that they also say *Thank you. Thanks very much*, or *Many thanks*.

*B* The owners of the objects say what they have 'lost', e.g. *I've lost my apple. Have you got it, please?* or *Is it in your bag, please? Is this it? No, that isn't mine, that's Dick's. Is this yours, Dick?* etc.

Or: *My friend Barbara has lost her scarf. Is it in your bag, please? Is this it? Is that yours, Barbara? No. No, it isn't here*, etc.

## 11 How?

Level **intermediate**
Age **children**
Group size **whole class**
Use **to practise adverbials of manner**

One learner goes out of the room and thinks of a simple action – such as cleaning the blackboard, drawing or writing something, counting objects or people, telling about what happened the day before, etc. Meanwhile the class has chosen an adverb of manner e.g. *quickly, slowly, softly, loudly*, etc. Back comes the one outside and performs the action in various ways until he hits on the manner chosen by the class and guesses the adverb. But he may

25

have to change the action to discover what the adverb is – one can hardly clean a blackboard loudly!

The class should respond to each 'performance' by using the adverb that seems appropriate to it, e.g. *No, it isn't 'quickly'*. If the 'performer' does not agree with their choice of adverb to describe the way he performs an action, he can say so, e.g. *I wasn't writing carelessly*.

It should not take long for any 'performer', by means of his actions to discover what adverb the class has chosen.

## Variant

As above, except that when the pupil outside returns, he performs no action but asks various members of the class to perform various actions: *Peggy, walk round the room! Charles, write something! Jane, pick up your pencil!* Those called upon must try to do what they are asked in the manner of the secret adverb; if this is impossible, they must say *I can't do what you ask*.

## 12 What **does** he/she want? (*or* What do they want?)

| | |
|---|---|
| Level | **elementary and intermediate** |
| Age | **children** |
| Group size | **whole class** |
| Use | **to practise 'I want somebody to do something'** |

Somebody (or more than one person) whispers something to the boy/girl/children in front, or writes something on a piece of paper, e.g. *Wash your hands. Go to the shops. Clean your bicycle. Brush your shoes. Comb your hair. Sing a song.* Once the game is understood, such commands can be contributed by the class. Then: *What does he/she/do they want me to do?* Guesses follow, e.g. *He/She/They want you to stand on a chair/leave the room*, etc. until a correct guess is made. *What does he/she want him/her/them to do?* is also possible, the question being asked by somebody else and the guesses being directed at this person.

At the right level of proficiency, commands of the type *Get your hair cut. Have your bicycle cleaned*, etc. can also be included.

## 13 Where are you off to? (*or* Where are you going?)

Level **intermediate**
Age **fairly young children**
Group size **whole class**
Use **to practise the infinitive of purpose.**

Somebody walks to the door and says *Goodbye, everybody, goodbye.* The class says: *Oh, where are you going?* Reply: *I'm off to/going to the supermarket/butcher's/stationer's/greengrocer's*, etc. Class: *What are you going there for?* or *Why are you going there?* Reply: *Guess (You must guess.)* Everybody guesses. *To buy a kilo of beans/a chair/a pint of milk/some potatoes*, etc. (choosing the vocabulary according to the kind of shop mentioned). Whenever a correct guess is made, the 'guesser' changes places with the 'shopper'.

## 14 The going to game: What am I going to draw/do/buy? etc.

Level **elementary and intermediate**
Age **any**
Group size **whole class**
Use **to practise 'going to' with reference to action in the immediate future**

This game can take various forms. For instance, somebody thinks of something that he or she is going to draw on the board, and the others guess either by asking *Are you going to draw a big house?* etc. or by stating *You're going to draw a big house*, etc. Responses: *No, I'm not going to draw a big house*, etc. and when the right guess is made: *Yes, that's right, I'm going to draw . . .*

Drawing is of course only one thing: there are all the other actions that can be performed or mimed singly or one after the other. Every language learner thinks of something to do, and keeps quiet about it. *Dick*, says the teacher. Dick comes forward. *Tell me what you're going to do.* Dick whispers it. *All right*, the

27

teacher says (or *No, think of something else*). *Now what's Dick going to do?* Answers are taken as hands go up. *He's going to sit on your chair/unlock the cupboard/sing a song/write his name on the board*, etc. *Is that what you're going to do, Dick? No.* Presently somebody guesses: *He's going to put the waste-paper-basket in that corner.* Dick: *Right, that's what I'm going to do.* Teacher: *All right, put it there, Dick.* Be sure to let him do it.

## Variant

*Where am I/is he*, etc, *going to put it?*, meaning any object small enough to be moved to various places. Answers make use of prepositional phrases, e.g. *You're going to put it behind the piano/on top of the cupboard/under those books*, etc.

The third person (and indirect speech) can be brought in with the help of a kind of 'triangular' arrangement. *What's he going to do? Ask him. Are you going to . . . , Dick? No, I'm not. He says he isn't going to . . . Ask him whether he's going to . . . Are you going to . . . , Dick? No, I'm not*, etc.

Don't forget the plurals. Two or more pupils can decide what they are going to do together, and the suggestions and responses will be *You're going to . . . Are you going to . . . ?* and *No, we're not./Yes, we are*, or *Ask them whether they are going to . . . , No, they aren't going to . . .* , etc.

## 15 You may have...

| | |
|---|---|
| Level | **intermediate and advanced** |
| Age | **any (but not young children)** |
| Group size | **whole class or groups** |
| Use | **to practise 'may have' + past participle and prepositional phrases** |

Leader: *I've lost my purse/ring/key*, etc. *Where can it be?* (or *Where could it be?* or *Where can/could it possibly be?* or *Where could I have dropped/left it?*) Suggestions, at least one from each member of the class: *You may have left it at home/in the bathroom/in the door*, etc. *You may have dropped it in the bus/in the train/on the road*, etc. The suggestions will vary according to the nature of the object and the circumstances, and so will the responses, e.g. *No, I don't think I did. I didn't come by bus/car/train this morning. I remember putting it on after visiting the bathroom. Oh no, I wouldn't throw it away – that would be silly*, etc.

## 16 Perhaps

| | |
|---|---|
| Level | **elementary, intermediate, and advanced (according to the language used)** |
| Age | **any** |
| Group size | **whole class** |
| Use | **to practise one use of the present continuous, past continuous, etc.** |

One of the learners goes out of sight and hearing and performs some action which has been written down beforehand, either by the teacher for him/her to see or by him/her for the teacher to see. Examples: *Go and wash your hands in the cloakroom* (or *I'm going to . . .*). *Get my coat from the car*, etc.

In this game the actions should be of a kind which can be performed and they should actually be carried out. An alternative although in some ways inferior procedure is for the 'doer' to write down secretly what he is 'doing' and then to remain in the room, so that others merely guess what is on the paper; but this is less interesting.

### Variants

*A Hidden actions*. Audible and continuous actions can be performed behind a big screen. They should be fairly easy to guess and everybody should have one ready to perform. *What's he/she doing? He's/She's sweeping the floor/counting money/winding up a watch*, etc.

*B Everybody pretends*. Everybody has a different mime to perform; nobody else knows what it is. Others guess as the mimes are performed, e.g. *He's/She's washing his/her face/brushing his/her teeth/writing a letter/answering the phone*, etc. However obvious the action is, there may often be a struggle to find the words needed to communicate, as one wishes to do, that one knows what it is and knows how to describe it.

With advanced learners a broad range of mimed actions is

possible: *sitting behind someone big at the cinema, trying to put the TV picture right, watching a tennis match* (side-to-side head movements), *cracking nuts, peeling a banana/apple/orange, eating spaghetti/ice-cream, trying to unlock a door with the wrong key, crossing a busy street, trying to get a taxi at a busy time, entering the sea when the water is cold, walking along a muddy/snowy street,* etc.

If the guesses are made after the mime has been done, the past continuous or present perfect continuous are appropriate, e.g. *He was looking for a seat on the bus,* etc.

C  This variant involves make-believe but not miming. One or two learners go outside for a minute and choose an activity, perhaps from a list. They then come back and ask: *What was I/were we doing while you were sitting here?* Guesses: *You were sailing a boat/climbing a mountain/swimming across the river/selling newspapers,* etc. The activities on the list should go with the learners' interests and experience of life.

Points can be scored for correct guesses, which can come from the teams in turn.

# 17  If it happened...

| | |
|---|---|
| Level | **intermediate and advanced** |
| Age | **any** |
| Group size | **whole class** |
| Use | **to practise conditional clauses (hypothetical)** |

While the class, with the teacher's help, is imagining something that might happen, one learner is out of the room. On returning, he or she asks various learners *What would you do if it happened?* until in due course it becomes clear what the imaginary event must be. Answers begin *I would . . .*

Examples
*a.  I would visit Britain/move to a bigger house/take my mother for a long holiday/give presents to all my friends,* etc. (Answers such as these would doubtless lead the questioner to guess *If you won a lot of money.*)
*b.  I would stay here/ring up home to ask somebody to come/take shelter in a shop/run home very quickly/borrow somebody's coat,* etc. (Such answers might bring the guess *If it began to rain hard.*)

Answers should be so worded that the secret is not given away immediately, as it would be, for instance, if an umbrella were mentioned in connection with *If it began to rain*.

Both possible and impossible 'happenings' may be allowed, and some of the answers are bound to be a bit improbable. The teacher's help should be directed towards ensuring that 'happenings' are chosen which enable as many suggestions as possible to be put forward.

## 18 Waiters

| | |
|---|---|
| Level | **elementary and intermediate** |
| Age | **children** |
| Group size | **whole class, teams** |
| Use | **to practise 'I'd like' and some of the vocabulary of meals** |

There are two teams, each of which chooses its 'waiter'. Everybody draws on a sheet of paper something which can be obtained at a café, e.g. a ham sandwich, a cup of tea, a glass of orange juice, a meat pie, bacon and eggs. At the side of each drawing the appropriate phrase is printed. The sets of papers are put in two piles on the table. The teams alternate in asking their 'waiters' for something to eat or drink: each child in the team asks for something different, e.g. *Could you bring me a roll and butter. I want/I'd like a boiled egg, please.* The waiter looks in his pile of drawings and if he can find the right one he takes it to the 'customer' and says *Here you are, sir/madam*; if he cannot find the drawing in the pile, he says *I'm sorry, sir/madam, we haven't got any rolls/eggs*, etc. The winning team is the one whose 'waiter' first succeeds in serving all his 'customers'.

As soon as a 'customer' has been served with something, he can order something else to go with it.

# 19 Hide and search

Level **intermediate**
Age **children**
Group size **whole class**
Use **to practise conditional clauses (factual or open condition) and the 'may' of possibility**

A small object, such as a button or coin, is hidden somewhere while the searcher waits outside. Converse with the rest of the class in this way: *What will Jim/Jane find/see if he/she looks in your desk/in Sally's bag/in the cupboard/under those papers/behind the stove?* etc. *He'll/She'll find four books and a ruler/some sandwiches/six piles of books and three bottles of ink*, etc.

Preliminary conversation might also involve the *may* of possibility. *What may he/she open/move/look behind? Where may he/she look?* At a more advanced stage *should* and *were* might be practised in the same situation: *If he should look in your desk, what would he find? If he were to move those books, what would he discover/see there?* etc.

The search may be for several objects, and there may be a number of searchers. The teacher need not know where the objects are – they can be placed by members of the class.

So Jim or Jane come back and search. As they search, teacher and class have a little conversation. *Where has Jim looked (so far)? Where is he going to look now? Has Jane looked under the table (yet)? Is she going to open the cupboard?* And so on. *Have you looked in my bag (yet), Jim?* But do not bother the searchers too much.

# 20 Where could ... have looked?

Level **intermediate and advanced**
Age **children**
Group size **whole class**
Use **to practise 'could/might have ...'**

This is an activity which follows upon the previous game. Everybody looks back at what has happened.

For instance: *Did Jim look in the cupboard, Alan? No, miss. Could he have looked there? Yes, he could, but he didn't. Where else could he have looked, but didn't look?* Everybody makes one suggestion. *He could have looked under my foot/behind that picture/in the vase*, etc. *Did you look under his foot/behind that picture*, etc. *Jim? No. Could you have looked there? Yes.* The class is talking about what they saw happen and not happen.

An alternative to *could* here is *might*.

# 21 If ... had looked ...

|  |  |
|---|---|
| Level | **intermediate and advanced** |
| Age | **children** |
| Group size | **whole class** |
| Use | **to practise conditional clauses (contrary to past fact) and adverbial clauses introduced by 'although', 'because', 'until', and 'when'** |

Once again, for example: *Did Jim look on top of the cupboard, Alan? No, he didn't. What's on top of the cupboard?* (or *What is there on the cupboard?*) *Have a look, Vera. Tell us what you see.* She does so. *Did Jim look there? No. What would he have found if he had looked there?* Vera's list is repeated.

And so on. The game has supplied the basis for a conversation using this type of conditional as a means of communication.

## Variants

These can make use of *although, when, because, until*, etc.

A   *Did Jane look in the drawer of this table? Yes, she did. And did she find the key? No, she didn't. But was the key there? Yes it was. It was there. Although it was there, she didn't see it. Why not? Because she didn't look properly? Because it was at the back? Perhaps ... Although he looked in your desk, Bill didn't find the button. Was it there? Yes. Why didn't he find it? Because it was inside a book/at the bottom*, etc.

B   *When did Harry find the watch? Did he find it when he looked in the pocket of my overcoat? No. Well, when did he find it? When he looked on the window-ledge.* And so on for other objects.

## 22 Alibi

| Level | **intermediate and advanced** |
|---|---|
| Age | **any (except young children)** |
| Group size | **whole class** |
| Time taken | **40–45 minutes** |
| Use | **to practise the simple past, past continuous, 'but', 'while', 'whereas', and reported speech** |

A crime has been committed – for instance, a local shop or bank was broken into one evening recently – and two people are suspected of the crime. They deny their guilt. They were together at the time, but not near the shop: they claim to have a perfect alibi.

All this is explained to the class and then two pupils are chosen as 'suspects'. They go outside and invent together a detailed story to account for their movements between, say, six and midnight on the evening of the crime. They must be able to say, for instance, where and when they met, what and whom they saw, what the weather was like, what they were wearing, where they went and how long they were there, what they were talking about, and so on. (They are not permitted, in the game, to stay at home reading – they must be out and about in the town or village, and doing various things.)

These two 'suspects' should be relatively good at English or whatever the foreign language is. Even so, it will take them five to ten minutes to make up a suitable story to establish their alibi (i.e. 'prove' that they were both elsewhere and doing something else at the time the crime was committed).

While they are outside, what do the others do? Teacher and class talk together about the sorts of questions they, representing the 'police', will put to the suspects when, one at a time, they re-enter the room: *Where did you meet your friend? At what time did you meet him? What was the weather like? Where did you go? How did you get there?* If they went to a cinema: *What did you pay for your seats? Did you sit upstairs or downstairs?* If they went to a café: *What did you eat?* And so on. Try to ensure that each member of the class has at least two questions ready to ask. ('Reminder' words and phrases can be put on the board.)

Then the first 'suspect' is called in and the 'interrogation' begins. The teacher should help with this, asking questions too and prompting the shyer and slower learners. The teacher should also make a brief note of some of the answers given. Most of the talking should be done by the class.

The first 'suspect' then leaves the room again and the second 'suspect' is called in. The same questions are asked, and some additional ones, and contradictions begin to appear between what the two 'suspects' have said about their doings. For instance, the first may have said that they had fish and chips in the cinema restaurant, the second that they had ice-cream elsewhere.

Re-questioning of the two 'suspects' together soon reveals all the points of difference between their stories, and the alibi breaks down. At this stage the class is asked to say whether the 'suspects' are 'guilty' or not, and those who say they are must give one reason for thinking so, e.g. *Philip said that they met by the café at the corner of the street, while/but/whereas Owen said they met outside the cinema.* The teacher helps the class to express the contradictions noticed, and thus certain patterns of reported speech, as well as uses of *but*, *while*, and *whereas* are practised.

The teacher's preparation should consist chiefly of visualizing the possibilities (where the 'suspects' could have gone, what they could have done, etc.) in considerable detail, and of getting the class to visualize these possibilities too and to ask a sufficient variety of questions. The teacher should also see where these questions will lead and what contradictions are likely to appear, and should remain aware also of the grammatical patterns, although these may not be commented on at the time.

## Variants

*A* If the crime has been committed in a house or office, all the residents or employees (i.e. possibly a large proportion of the class) have to answer questions and give a convincing account of their movements, etc. Discrepancies emerge in the same way.

*B* Instead of being questioned successively, the two (or more) suspects can be questioned simultaneously by different groups, each asking the same questions. When the groups come together afterwards, the different answers given can be compared and the contradictions brought out[3].

*C* The 'suspects', after conferring, can separately make *written* statements describing their whereabouts, etc on the evening of the crime. These are mimeographed and copies are given to all members of the class, which prepares (perhaps in groups) written questions for use in the oral interrogation. This is a more time-consuming procedure, but in some ways it enhances the value of the game.Certainly the questions are likely to be more penetrating, especially if they have also been discussed orally with the teacher before the 'suspects' enter.

## Notes and references

1 This is a simple version of a very old game played in the British Isles. See *Children's Games in Street and Playground* by Iona and Peter Opie, pp. 290–92.
2 These three variants are adapted from *Faites Vos Jeux* by M. Buckby and D. Grant.
3 With acknowledgements to J. M. M. Horwood.

# Chapter 2
# VOCABULARY
# GAMES

*A vocabulary game is one in which the learners' attention is focused mainly on words. Many of the games in other chapters, where the main focus of attention is elsewhere, give incidental vocabulary practice. Up to a point spelling games (Chapter 3) may be looked upon as vocabulary games.*

## 1 What's this/that?
## Who's this/that?

|  |  |
|---|---|
| Level | **elementary** |
| Age | **children** |
| Group size | **whole class or groups** |
| Use | **to practise naming people and objects** |

Learners in turn hold up or touch or point to objects or people (or to pictures of them), naming a pupil in another team to answer. Those who answer correctly ask a similar question in return. If an answer is incorrect, the questioner (or perhaps someone else from the same team) asks another question. A point may be scored for every correct question answered.

Replies take the form *It's a . . . It's the . . . It's my/your/his/her . . . It's X. They're . . . and . . . Yes, it is. No, they aren't. No, I'm . . .*, etc.

At a slightly less elementary stage a game can be made out of the following kind of naming sequence: A (to B): *What's this?*, B: *It's a . . .* A (to class or group): *Is it a . . . ?* Reply: *Yes/No.*

'Choice' questions also lend themselves to this game: *Is this a lemon or an orange?*

## 2 Shopping

Level **elementary and intermediate**
Age **any**
Group size **small class or groups**
Use **to practise the vocabulary needed for various kinds of shopping**

There are many vocabulary games of this type. They can be adapted to circumstances. Examples:

A *My father/sister /I/You and I*, etc. *went to* (name a town). *Oh yes, did he/she/you? What did he/she/you bring back? He/She/I/We brought back* . . . Each learner adds an item and repeats the items already mentioned by other learners. If this is found unduly difficult, write some of the items on the board. Keep a note of what is mentioned. In a large class the list becomes unbearably long and the game is then better played in groups.

B *I went to the market/shops/supermarket with* . . . *and there we bought* . . . , etc. The vocabulary can be restricted to what is obtainable at one kind of shop, and this varies from country to country.

C Amounts can be specified: *I went shopping yesterday and bought a dozen eggs, a pound/half a kilo of coffee, a pound of butter*, etc.

D Other tenses can be used: *My mother and sister have gone to* . . . *What are they going to buy? Guess* . . . *Every Saturday we go shopping, and what do you think we buy?* etc.

E 'Uncountables' and 'countables' may need practice: *some rice, some cheese, some bacon, two packets of rice, a quarter of bacon, six eggs*, etc.

## 3 Shopping lists

Level **intermediate**
Age **any**
Group size **whole class or groups**
Use **to brush up the vocabulary of shopping**

This game can be based on a clear map showing where various shops are in part of a town. If this is not a real town known to the learners, it could be similar.

Each member of the class is given a different shopping list and has to say where he or she would go to get the things listed and how he or she would get there, e.g. *I'd take a No. 6 bus and get off at Bell Corner. I'd go to the supermarket first and buy the groceries – a pound of butter, a jar of coffee, some radishes, a cucumber, and some cheese – and also a packet of envelopes and a writing pad, or I could get those at the stationer's on the opposite side of the street. On the same side as the stationer's I could visit the baker's further along the street and get a loaf of bread and some rolls. I'd go to the chemist's next door to get a tube of toothpaste, a lipstick, and some throat tablets . . .* And so on. The 'shoppers' would be given a chance to study their lists first and decide where to go. The teacher could interrupt and ask *Who else has to/needs to/wants to visit the chemist's?* etc. *Nobody has been to the sports shop yet. What's on your list, X? Which shops do you want to go to? No, you can't get sweets at the baker's,* etc.

Although such a game might be based on shopping possibilities anywhere, it could if necessary serve the purpose of teaching the class something about everyday life in a country speaking the foreign language concerned.

## 4 Look at what we bought

|  |  |
|---|---|
| Level | **intermediate and advanced** |
| Age | **any** |
| Group size | **whole class or groups** |
| Use | **to brush up the vocabulary of shopping** |

*I/We went to London* (or *New York*, or somewhere else) *. . . and there I bought a tie, a necklace, a handkerchief, a hat, a TV set, a tennis racket, a suit, a pair of shoes, a box of chocolates,* etc.

But the objects are not mentioned, they are mimed. The mimes should not be superficial or hurried, but properly thought out and then performed in such a way that everybody has a good chance of guessing what they represent.

The words (*a tie, a necklace,* etc.) are written on the board as the correct guesses are made, and each player repeats the sentence and all the mimes before adding his or her own.

Other objects for miming: a piano, a guitar, a cat (miaows permitted), a bed (mime sleeping), a bicycle, a mirror (mime looking into it, making up, etc.), some butter (spread it), a football (mime the shape and also kicking), a writing-pad, a pack of cards, a shaver, some perfume, a camera, etc.

# 5 Classroom shop

| | |
|---|---|
| Level | **intermediate** |
| Age | **children** |
| Group size | **whole class or groups** |
| Use | **to practise the vocabulary of shopping** |

The pupils provide the articles for sale – or pictures, drawings, or models of them, or simply their names on cards – and the teacher, to get the game going, acts first as salesman and then as a customer. Useful phrases: *Can I help you? Have you got a ...? Have you got any ...? I want to buy ... pounds/kilograms of ... Please give me ... How much is (all) that? Is that right?* (when handing over the exact money), *I'm sorry we're out of stock/we haven't got that*, etc.

# 6 Going away

| | |
|---|---|
| Level | **elementary and intermediate** |
| Age | **children (variant B: young children)** |
| Group size | **whole class or groups** |
| Use | **to brush up some of the vocabulary of journeys and holidays and one use of 'will'** |

This can be *Going abroad* or *Going to London/Vienna/Los Angeles* or wherever you like, or *Packing my bag* or *Packing for a holiday* or *My Auntie Jennifer went on holiday* or whatever seems most suitable – and the game need not always be played in the same way. Let us take the first idea.

No. 1: *I'm going abroad and I will take a suitcase with me.*

No. 2: *I'll take a suitcase and a camera.*

No. 3: *I'll take a suitcase, a camera, and some films.*

And so on, each repeating the previous items and adding one of his or her own.

# 7 Aunt Mary's cat[1]

| | |
|---|---|
| Level | **intermediate and advanced** |
| Age | **any** |
| Group size | **whole class or groups** |
| Use | **a vocabulary stretcher (adjectives and adverbs)** |

This is an old party game played by children and adults together, the adults usually saying whether the word chosen is possible or not. Again, the name can be varied: *My uncle's parrot. The grocer's horse. Bill Lee's bulldog. My grandmother's monkey*, etc. The first player begins with *a* and says perhaps *My aunt Mary's cat is an alarming cat*. The second has to use an adjective beginning with *b*, e.g. *My aunt Mary's cat is a bad cat*. The third may continue *My aunt Mary's cat is a careful cat*. And so on through the alphabet.

Adverbs can be added to adjectives: *My aunt Mary's cat is an alarmingly fierce/badly behaved/carefully fed/dangerously thin cat*, etc. Or: . . . *is alarmingly fierce*, etc.

## Variant

*I know a cat* (or possibly *a boy/girl/man/woman* or something else) *named* (or *whose name is*) *Archie/Anne*, etc. *It/He/She lives in America and is able*, etc. This is more difficult, calling for a considerable vocabulary.

# 8 Incomplete definitions

| | |
|---|---|
| Level | **intermediate and advanced** |
| Age | **any (except young children)** |
| Group size | **whole class and groups** |
| Use | **to practise how to describe things they know** |

A member of one team defines something and challenges somebody in the other team to guess what it is. Team points are given for correct guesses, and an extra point if the word is spelt correctly.

Much depends on what is chosen for definition, and also on

not giving away too much. For example, *an elephant* can be defined as a large animal which lives in India and Africa and which can carry people as well as goods – but do not mention its trunk, which would make it too easy to guess.

Examples: A piece of furniture in which we keep clothes (*a wardrobe*). A way of telling us to stop or go ahead in the street (*traffic lights*). A place where a farmer keeps his cows (*a cattle shed*). A means of sending a spoken message a long way (*the telephone*).

# 9 I spy

Level **elementary**
Age **children**
Group size **whole class or groups**
Use **to brush up known vocabulary**

This is an old and simple vocabulary game. Somebody says:

> *I spy*
> *With my little eye*
> *Something beginning with B.*

Others guess what the object is. Susan: *The blackboard? No, not the blackboard.* Dick: *A biscuit? No, I can't see a biscuit.* Stephen: *Dick's ball? Yes, that's right, Dick's ball.* It then becomes Stephen's turn. He thinks of something beginning with another letter, e.g. S. *I spy . . . something beginning with S.* The object must be visible in the room or in a wall picture.

If anyone dislikes *spy* because it is not among the ten thousand most frequent words in printed English or because of its associations, then the following rhyme can be substituted:

> *One – two – three,*
> *What can I see?*
> *Something in this room* (or *garden*)
> *Beginning with . . .*

## 10 Coffee-pot

Level **intermediate**
Age **any**
Group size **whole class and groups**
Use **to brush up vocabulary: food, drink, clothing, tools, etc.**

This is usually played as a vocabulary game. Somebody thinks of an object and others ask questions such as *Where do you keep your coffee-pot? Is your coffee-pot big? What is your coffee-pot made of? Can we see your coffee-pot in the room? Can we eat your coffee-pot? Do you wear your coffee-pot?* Both *yes-no* questions and *wh*-questions can be asked.

The *coffee-pot* may be almost anything – somebody's TV set, somebody's stamp album, the local railway station, the post office, the teacher's hat, somebody's bicycle, your shoes, the moon, etc.

*Coffee-pot* can also stand for a verb, and the questions might include *Can everybody coffee-pot? Do you coffee-pot very often? Where do you go to coffee-pot?* etc. Almost any action verb is possible here, e.g. *dance, sing, swim, go for a walk, climb,* etc.

## 11 Shipwreck lists

Level **intermediate**
Age **any**
Group size **whole class and groups**
Use **to brush up the vocabulary of food, drink, clothing, tools, etc.**

Each group has pencil and paper and the group leader does the writing. First, the names of foods must be written down. Allow two or three minutes for all the groups to do this, then ask for drinks, and finally for articles of clothing.

Group A leader reads out Group A's list, while the other group leaders cross out on their lists anything he mentions. Then Group B leader reads out what his group still has, and the other groups cross out those items if they have them, and so on with all the groups. The result will be that the items not crossed out on any list will be those that only that group has thought of. *You have been wrecked on a desert island, and this is all the food and drink and clothing you have.* The surviving items are read out. The group with the longest list (including no doubt one or two items that would not be essential or even suitable on the island) is the winner.

## 12 Picture squares

|          |                                              |
|----------|----------------------------------------------|
| Level    | **intermediate**                             |
| Age      | **any**                                       |
| Group size | **whole class and groups**                 |
| Use      | **to brush up the vocabulary of food, drink, etc.** |

Each member of the class has a grille like this:

| 1 | 2 |
|---|---|
| **3** | **4** |
| **5** | **6** |

or with a larger number of squares. Distribute pictures of, say, food and drink, and things to do with cooking, eating, and drinking. These pictures have been drawn or have been cut out of catalogues and journals: they will be of different sizes. Each picture is numbered, although some pictures bear the same number. A set of, say, twelve pictures is given to each group. The group passes them round and everybody writes the name of as many pictures as possible in the spaces of his own grille: the number of the picture should correspond to the number of the space, e.g. a *loaf of bread* (2), *a saucepan* (4), *a knife and fork* (1), *egg and chips* (3). Members of the group can help one another. The first group to have something written – correctly and neatly – in every space of everybody's grille is the winner.[2]

## Variant

The pictures and vocabulary may belong to other topics, e.g. the contents of a house (furniture, wall decorations, etc.), transport (aircraft, trains, road vehicles), camping (tents, cooking utensils, equipment, etc.), toys, sports, clothing, and so on. It depends on the learners' concerns and interests.

# 13 Remembering

|   |   |
|---|---|
| Level | **elementary** |
| Age | **children** |
| group size | **whole class** |
| Use | **familiarization with known vocabulary; spelling practice** |

Simple sketches are drawn on the board. If you have a long stretch of board there can be several 'artists' drawing at once: they can be, for instance, three learners from each of two teams. As soon as they have finished, they print neatly under each drawing what it is supposed to be (*a chicken, a tree, an aeroplane,* etc.). The class is given a few moments to look at these words, then the teacher rubs them out and the class writes them from memory, looking at the drawings (some of which would no doubt be unrecognizable if one had not been told what they were). Then other learners come forward to draw and name other things, and the procedure is repeated. With a quick class this can be done three or four times. The team with the most words right, legible, and correctly spelt is the winner.[3]

## Variant

There is a pile of cut-out pictures or drawings on cards on the tables. Two or three learners from each team quickly choose one, stick it on the board with blu-tack or a similar adhesive, and print underneath it on the board the name of the object(s). The same procedure is then followed.

The vocabulary field can of course be restricted.

# 14 Word-race

Level **elementary and intermediate**
Age **any (depending on the picture)**
Group size **groups**
Use **familiarization with known vocabulary; spelling practice**

Each group has the same picture, which should be similar to but not identical with one the class has seen before: for example, a river scene with a different person falling into the water, different trees, different boats and people in them. In five minutes (or whatever time seems appropriate) each group has to write down legibly and correctly the names of as many things visible in the pictures as possible, e.g. *two canoes, a fisherman, a barking dog, a cyclist, a small boy in the water* . . .

# 15 Shopping expedition[4]

Level **advanced**
Age **children**
Group size **groups**
Use **familiarization with known words connected with shopping**

There is a story-teller, who tells a simple story about something (e.g. *My friend Freddy/Freda*) who went shopping. The other members of the class or group represent different shops (the baker's, the grocer's, the toyshop, the stationer's) Freddy or Freda might visit. Unless one is trying to convey an impression of everyday urban life in an English speaking country, these should be the sort of shops the learners are familiar with. (Alternatively, the learners may represent different departments in a big store.)

Every time the story-teller mentions a shop, he says that the shopper wanted to buy something beginning with (here he gives a letter of the alphabet). The learner representing the shop must then mention something sold at his shop which begins with that letter. For example, if the letter is *m* the greengrocer could say *a melon*, the butcher *mutton*, the grocer *a pot of marmalade*, the toyshop *a monkey*, the fishmonger *a mackerel*, and so on. To keep the game going at a reasonable pace, the story-teller can slowly count up to ten while the shopkeeper is thinking. Often there will be no answer, and no point will be gained, but if anyone can fill in the gap while 1–10 is counted again, that will be a point for him.

# 16  Old Macdonald (*or* Macdougall)

This song, which all ages like singing, is a lively reminder of farmyard vocabulary – and the name of almost any domestic or farm animal can be worked in.

> Old Macdonald had a farm,
> E-I-E-I-O,
> And on that farm he had some ducks,
> E-I-E-I-O,
> With a quack-quack here
> And a quack-quack there,
> Here a quack, there a quack,
> Everywhere a quack-quack,
> Old Macdonald had a farm,
> E-I-E-I-O.

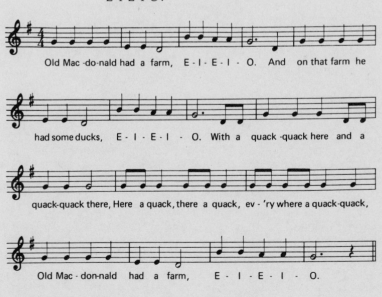

Old Mac -do-nald had a farm, E - I - E - I - O. And on that farm he had some ducks, E - I - E - I - O. With a quack -quack here and a quack-quack there, Here a quack, there a quack, ev - 'ry where a quack-quack, Old Mac - don-nald had a farm, E - I - E - I - O.

In other verses *Old Macdonald* had a dog (bow-wow), a cow (moo-moo), some geese (hissing sounds), some turkeys (gobble-gobble), some bees (buzzing sounds), some sheep (bleating sounds), some pigs (grunting sounds), etc.

## Notes and references

1 A detailed description of this game will be found in *English Language Teaching*, XIV, 1: Pattern Practice, or 'The Parson's Cat' by R. A. Close.
2 Adapted from *Guide de l'Assistant de Français* by G. Fontier and M. le Cunff, p. 90.
3 Adapted from *Stories, Plays, and Games* by R. Hellyer-Jones and P. Lampater.
4 From *Games for Children while Travelling* by Sid Hedges.

# Chapter 3
# SPELLING GAMES

*It is a half-truth that spelling can be picked up. Voracious readers are often good spellers, but not always; nor does every language learner read voraciously! A wisely planned foreign language course provides for drills and exercises to ensure that spelling is mastered. Fortunately these are readily converted into games.*

*A few general principles are worth observing.*

*A lot depends on the visual image of the whole word, which tends to be photographed on the memory. Thus the visual image should never, if we can avoid it, be an incorrect one. Do not write up misspellings on the board and do not allow a misspelt word any pupil has written there to remain – rub it out. Refrain also from giving the class words of which the letters have been put in the wrong order – they can only sort them out correctly if they know how to spell the word, and in the process of trying to do so are likely to be confused by several incorrect versions.*

*Spelling games ought not to be played as if they were only tests. Every spelling game should include or follow a period of study – of the words used in the game.*

*Words are best introduced to the class in the context of sentences. To focus on the spelling, it is necessary to list them out of context now and then, but not for long. Words like* their *and* there, wait *and* weight, *should always be put into a phrase.*

*There is little point in including words which the class in general can spell easily.*

*Spelling exercises and games are not so much needed at an elementary stage, when the learners have seen relatively few words, as later, when they may have seen many. A brief spelling game twice a week (if there are several weekly lesson periods) is probably enough, but a hard-and-fast rule cannot be laid down.*

*The ability to* write *the word is the main thing. The first writing is the copying from the board or book of short and fully meaningful sentences, with the meaning of which the learners have become familiar in oral communication. There is no reason to spell these out orally.*

*If the foreign language alphabet is the same as the mother tongue alphabet, the letter names need not be taught until writing is well under way. It is another matter if the foreign language alphabet is an entirely different one. Then we must give handwriting (i.e. letter forming and letter linking) instruction, and the learners might as well meet with the letter names along with the new letters themselves. But even then there should not be a divorce of what is visually learnt from what has been learnt orally. These new and strange letters make up the short sentences the learners have already been speaking, and can be 'found', with the teacher's help, in the visual forms of such sentences.*

*The games which follow are roughly grouped according to type, beginning with easy ones. They can be played with almost any kind of class. There is overlap with vocabulary games, so that some could be classified under either heading.*

*Note: As the use of all the games that follow is to practise spelling, this will not be stated before each game.*

## 1 Write what you see

| | |
|---|---|
| Level | **elementary and intermediate** |
| Age | **children** |
| Group size | **whole class** |

Straightforward copying is the simplest kind of spelling activity, but even this can be done in a variety of ways.

1.1   If there is a list of words on the board, or, better still, a continuous piece of reading, one team copies the words underlined in green and another those underlined in red: one set of words should not be harder than the other. Points will be given for accurate copying.

1.2   Somebody from each team in turn underlines or rings in the text a word for the others to copy. They copy this word at once. Exchange of papers or books between teams for correction: each team will be anxious to detect the other's mistakes. The teacher should make spot-checks.

1.3   The learners copy as in 1.1, or 1.2, exchange papers, etc. They then cover up what they have written. The teacher (or a learner) then rubs out the words one by one and as he does so the learners write them from memory. Then they uncover the hidden words and correct any mistakes, rewriting a misspelt word several times. Finally they exchange books once again for a final check as the teacher puts the words again on the board.

1.4 The class studies words and copies them. Then the teacher (or a learner) begins to rub out one word after another, and the learners have to guess which one is about to be rubbed out. They then tick it off on their list. The 'rubber-out' should keep the class puzzled and amused by, for instance, pretending to be on the point of rubbing out one word and then moving suddenly to another. (For young children.)

1.5 The teacher gives a number of words orally, one by one or a few at a time, and the learners find them in a dictionary and copy them. None of the words – which can be given in phrases or short sentences, so that meaning is not overlooked – should be absolutely new to them. Finally they are written on the board and papers exchanged.

1.6 *Kim's Word-Game*. This is a variant of Kim's Game, in which one tries to remember a group of small objects exposed to view for a short time. The class is shown a list of words (perhaps half a dozen) for a minute or two, with or without comment on features of the spelling – that depends on what the words are. The learners then write down as many as they can remember. If the words are presented in phrases, they can be asked to write the whole phrase.

The words can be written on the board and concealed by pinning a sheet of paper over them or turning the board round; or they can be shown on a flannelboard or a large card.

A fixed time is allowed for writing and then the words are shown again. The learners count, and correct if necessary, those they have written down, and add those missed.

## 2 Write what you hear

Level **elementary, intermediate, and advanced**
Age **any (especially children)**
Group size **whole class and groups**

2.1 A short list of words which have been giving difficulty is first studied, with or without the teacher's help. The teacher calls a word, names someone from each team, and says *Go*. (Alternatively, the learners come forward in some prearranged order.) These learners each write the word on the board. The first to finish correctly and legibly wins a point.

The others will watch keenly what their team member is doing, but they can also write the words down.

Rub out at once any mistake made on the board and put the spelling right. Don't say *Look at that, what's wrong with it?*

If the board is a wide expanse, two or three from each team can be writing on it at the same time.

This game is unsuitable for those who cannot write firmly or clearly enough on the board; young children find it hard to do so.

2.2   As in 2.1, except that everybody writes down the words dictated by the teacher or a learner – on paper. Self-correction is more convenient than exchange if the teacher is putting the words on the board one by one as the contest proceeds. Probably a combination of self-correction and mutual correction is best: first, the learners correct their own efforts, put at the bottom the number of marks they think they are entitled to, and write out five times any words they have misspelt; and then the members of another team check the accuracy of what they have done, the checker printing his initials at the end. The teacher's spot-check is essential. If this contest is held as a form of small group activity, the members of each group have to show the group leader what they have written as the activity proceeds, or the leader has to spell out each word. Points are scored by individuals, or there is no scoring; or papers may be exchanged for marking by other groups.

2.3   *What's your word?* Learners choose words (from a limited but fairly extensive list) with which to challenge one another. The teacher chooses the first challenger and everyone writes down the word he says. The challenger then puts it on the board (or the teacher does so) and names the next challenger.

Challengers may come in turn from different teams. Everybody writes the words, but the score is not counted for the challenger's team.

The game can of course be purely oral, and can be played by groups simultaneously.

2.4   *Second tries.* Certain words are studied and are then dictated by the teacher or learners to the class as a whole or to teams. Correction is made and the words are re-studied. Then they are dictated once more, possibly by a learner who has got them all correct, and this time there should be no mistakes at all. If any learners have a word wrong at both attempts, the game is too hard for them or preparation has been too short.

It is a good thing for the learners to keep their own personal lists of words they have found hard to spell, crossing them off as they prove they have mastered them.

An effective device for measuring spelling improvement is the *thermometer*, which is simply a vertical line every learner rules in his book. Every time a spelling test is given the learner marks the number of mistakes on the 'thermometer' (preferably in red) and puts the date of the test underneath. The idea is to get one's 'temperature' down to normal, so 'no mistakes' should be equated with 37°C (98°F). Those with numerous mistakes suffer from *Spelling Fever*.

2.5  The teacher dictates a short passage – an anecdote, for instance – but the class does not write it all down. Only certain words are written, which the teacher indicates by speaking them a little more loudly, or by repeating them, or in some other way. The passage should first be read aloud normally, so that everybody knows what it is about, and then dictated sense group by sense group, a pause being made after every word which has to be written down. The chosen words, in the phrases where they occur, are written on the board afterwards.

# 3  Write what you know

Level **intermediate**
Age **any**
Group size **whole class, teams, groups**

3.1  Riddles and definitions are suited chiefly to vocabulary work, but if they are simple, and the answer is to be written, it is a matter less of vocabulary knowledge than of knowing how to spell, and this sort of approach to spelling links it with experience of communication.

A teacher or learner says, for example, *Write down the name of something we hold over our heads when it rains.* The others perhaps write *umbrella*, or better, *an umbrella. And now something that we can wear when it rains. A raincoat. What do we call very heavy rain? A downpour.*

Preferably, except at a very advanced stage, the vocabulary should belong to the topic the class has been reading or writing about recently. It is best for the questions to follow on from one another, and not to be on completely different topics. The answer-words should be painstakingly selected beforehand.

Further examples: *What has four legs and a back but no head? (A chair.) What has a face and hands but no eyes? (A clock.) What has teeth but no mouth? (A comb.)*

3.2 The teacher (or a learner) says or writes up a word, e.g. *ball*, and the learners are given a limited time (say, five minutes) to put down words similar in form, e.g. *call, tall, fall, hall*. One then reads out what he has written and the others tick off on their lists the words mentioned and are asked what additional words they have. These too are read out and ticked off. A team or group contest is possible if for a particular pattern (e.g. *-all, un-, dis-*) plenty of words are obtainable. The one with the greatest number of different words wins a point.

## Variant

After the learners have written down their words, each (the teams alternating) reads out one word only. Everybody else ticks off these words, or if necessary adds them to his list. A note is kept of the number of words supplied by each team. There comes a point when, say, Team B can supply no more words, but members of the other teams can. Finally, perhaps, only one of the teams can supply another word, and that team, having the greatest number of different words, is the winner.

# 4 Stop

Level **elementary and intermediate**
Age **any (except young children)**
Group size **whole class, teams, or groups**

Somebody thinks of a word and indicates the number of letters in it by means of dashes on the board. The others each guess, asking such questions as *Is there a T in it?* If there is, the letter T is put in its correct place in the word. *Is there a B?* And so on.

If the letter suggested is not in the word, it is written at the side of the board and crossed out. Thus, if the word thought of is *table*, an S would be written at the side as $. At the same time the first line of the sign is drawn – it can be completed in exactly ten lines. Every time a wrong letter is suggested, a line is added to this drawing. When the STOP sign is complete, the team or group concerned has to stop playing. The last survivor wins the game.

It may be necessary to explain the procedure beforehand in the mother tongue.

## 5 Filling the gaps

| | |
|---|---|
| Level | **elementary** |
| Age | **young children** |
| Group size | **whole class or groups** |

Every learner has a number of cards, each bearing a letter clearly visible anywhere in the room. Each team can have cards of one colour, different from the other teams' colours. The letters which occur most often in printed English are *e, a, t, o, n, i, s, h, d, l*, and *r*, and each learner should have plenty of these; nobody should be given only letters of low frequency.

Think of a word (not too short) and ask for certain of the letters in it. Place the learners who have these letters in order, but leave gaps for the letters missing. The class has to guess the word and those with the missing letters then come forward to fill the gaps. Thus if the letters provided are *i, r,* and one *f* and the correct guess *giraffe* is made, the teacher says *Yes, good, it's giraffe*, and shows a picture of one. *Now, what's the first letter? Right, G. Who has a G? Harry, you were first. Come here. Where are you going to stand? Right. What's the next letter. A? No, A doesn't come next. Where does A come? Yes, Peter, stand next to F,* and so on. The letters are not necessarily taken in sequence.

## Variant

Each learner writes down on a slip of paper the names of, say, ten objects clearly visible in the classroom or in a classroom picture, or through the window, but with some of the letters missing, for instance all but the first and last. Dictionaries or word lists (preferably the latter) may be used. Papers are exchanged between teams or groups, the game being to guess what the words are and to fill in the missing letters. After a few minutes the lists are returned to their owners, who count up the number of correct solutions and put a mark at the bottom, and also write in the unsolved words. The papers are then exchanged as before and points are awarded to those with the fewest mistakes.

# 6  Word-completion

Level  **elementary and intermediate**
Age  **children (possibly also adults)**
Group size  **whole class, teams, groups**

A number of incomplete words, either in sentences or with a simple 'clue' attached to them, e.g. *a be---r (begs)*, are on the board. The pupils complete them on paper and if the teacher doubts their ability to do so without mistakes he allows them to consult the textbook or dictionary. The first to finish helps other members of his group or team. A limited time is allowed.

Even if the completion is made orally, it is helpful to write the words as well.

## Variants

*A  Word-race.* If there are two teams and two sets of identical words on the board, a learner from each team can go to the board and complete the first word in each set. These two run back to their seats as soon as they have finished and are replaced by another two and so on. The first team to complete all the words is the winner. There should be enough words to give everybody a turn. Written completion on paper can *precede* this relay race, which, if the words are neither too hard nor too easy for the class, is always exciting and enjoyable.

*B* One learner writes down a word secretly, but tells the others how many letters there are in it (so that they mark their papers with the appropriate number of dashes) and also give clues. For instance, if the word is UNIVERSITIES (12 letters) he can give three clues in succession – letters 7, 8, and 9 spell the opposite of *stand* (the others write in – SIT –); letters 9, 10, 11, and 12 spell something that many men wear (they add TIES and get SITIES); and the first two letters are short for United Nations. At this point somebody may guess the word and so will have to think of another.

# 7 Word-cards and letter-cards

Level **elementary and intermediate**
Age **children (possibly also adults)**
Group size **whole class, teams, groups**

7.1 Word-cards and letter-cards come in useful for word-completion games. Groups or individuals are given six or more cards each bearing a word with letters missing. They are also given a supply of letter-cards to complete the words, and this they do by placing the appropriate letter-cards over the blank spaces. The first learner or group to complete all the words gains a point.

## Variant

An alternative way of playing this is for the teacher to hold up the word-cards one by one or to write the words one by one on the board. Learners then find the right word-card in their set and proceed to complete it. When they have done so, they call *Ready* or put up their hands. A point is awarded for the first correct answer. Then the next word is shown and so on. This is a good procedure when the learners are unaccustomed to working on their own, but the teacher must go at the right pace for the class.

7.2 All the learners have three or four cards, each bearing a clearly drawn letter about 4 cms high. Each team can have its own colour of card. It is unnecessary for every member of a team to have all the letters of the alphabet, but to have nothing but letters which are rarely wanted is disappointing. In English the letters which most frequently occur are *e, a, t, o, n, i, s, h, d, l,* and *r.*

A word is called out or written on the board. (It is easier if the word is written, for then the learners have only to look at it to decide whether they can take part.) Every learner who has one of the letters in the word runs to the front and forms the word with other members of his team. They all hold up their letter-cards, and the first team ready scores a point.

If more than one learner in a team has a certain letter, as will often be the case, the one to get to the front first will join in making the word and any others will sit down again or stand aside; alternatively, they can stand behind another member of their own team who is holding the same letter. To 'compensate' those learners who sit at the back of the classroom and who will always tend to be the last to reach the front, letters of most frequent occurrence (e.g. *e, a, t, o, n, i*) can be given out more generously to them.

The class must be told beforehand exactly where the members of each team are to stand when forming their word.

## Variants

*A* Another way of playing this game is to let groups form their own words and show them to the class as soon as they are ready. As each word is formed, everybody else writes it down and says it as well.

Additionally, the opposite of a word just shown may be asked for, and the first group ready with it gets a point; or a noun to go with an adjective and vice versa, although the grammatical terms may not be used. Thus with *heavy* can go *bag*, or *weight*, with *stone* can go *sharp* or *small*, etc., these words being formed without having been suggested by the teacher.

*B* A group from each team stands in the front and a letter-card is given to each member in such a way that both (or all) groups can form the same word. The teacher should not say what the word is.

7.3 As soon as a word has been formed, as under 7.2, the class can be asked to 'photograph' it in their memories. *Have you all taken a photograph/photo/snap?* or *Have you all got it now? Yes. Then shut your eyes – shut them tightly and don't look – John, you're looking.* The teacher whispers to one or more of the children in the word *Turn round now*, so that they face away from the class and their letters cannot be seen. *All right, open your eyes. Who can tell me the missing letters? Hands up . . . Mary? Peter? . . . Yes, that's right. Now each of you go and tell one 'letter' to turn round again. Shut your eyes, everybody.*

Other variants will be found in the chapter on structure games.

# 8  Stepping-stones

Level     **elementary**
Age     **young children**
Group size     **whole class**

A river is drawn on the board and the task is to cross it by the stepping-stones. For each stone a word has to be spelt. If it is spelt correctly it is printed on the stone; if incorrectly, it is not written and the team makes no progress.

Words can be given to children of different teams in turn, but then there should be more than one drawing or at least more than one set of stepping-stones.

Some classes are lucky enough to have a lot of space, and can draw stepping-stones on the ground or floor, where there is a river full of crocodiles or other dangerous creatures ready to eat you up if you do not spell properly! Children hold the word-cards of the words they have spelt as they cross to the other side.

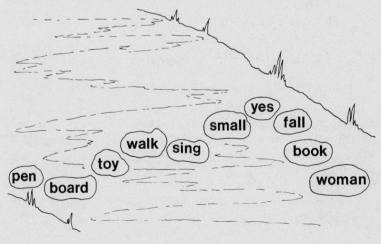

## Variants

Ladders can be drawn leaning against a house or tower, and the first player or team to reach the top is the winner. Each rung of the ladder is mounted by spelling a word, and the words are written between the rungs.

The idea of Jack and the Beanstalk can also be adapted for this purpose. Other possibilities: Skyscrapers (ascending one floor for every word), Journey to the Moon (10,000 kilometres or miles for each word), Crossing the Desert, etc.

# 9 Wolves and lambs

Level **elementary and intermediate**
Age **young children**
Group size **teams, groups**

The teams or groups sit in circles well apart from each other, and are visited by 'wolves' (or 'tigers' or 'lions' or some other animal if you like) from other teams. Each 'wolf' has a list of words to be spelt, and fear is shown as he approaches. Anyone who cannot spell the word the 'wolf' gives him has to stand aside as a captive 'lamb'. After a short time the 'shepherd' (the teacher) chases the 'wolves' away and they take their 'captives' back to their own groups. The team with the most 'captives' is the winner.

# 10 Scrabble, Lotto, etc.

Level **elementary, intermediate, and advanced**
Age **any**
Group size **pairs, groups, or whole class**

Excellent spelling practice is provided by certain popular board games such as *Scrabble* and *Lotto*. Here are a few simplified versions suitable now and then for the language lesson. They are also suitable for 'Language Club' or end-of-term activities (see Chapter 9b, p. 159).

10.1 *Classroom word-squares*. Everybody has a square, ruled into (say) 36 smaller squares. Someone calls out a succession of letters and the learners put each of these, as they are called, in one of their small squares, and try to build words they know, both down and across. Thus if the first 12 letters called are E, T, U, A, P, Q, M, E, R, S, F, and Y, three different players' squares might look like this:

**A**

|   |   | S |   |   |   |
|---|---|---|---|---|---|
| T | E | A | P |   |   |
|   |   | F |   |   |   |
| Q | U | E | R | Y |   |
|   |   |   |   |   |   |
| M |   |   |   |   |   |

**B**

|   |   |   |   |   | M |
|---|---|---|---|---|---|
| P |   | F |   |   |   |
| E | A | R | S |   |   |
| T |   |   |   |   |   |
|   | Q |   | E | U |   |
|   |   | Y |   |   |   |

**C**

| T | E |   |   | F |   |
|---|---|---|---|---|---|
|   |   |   | Q | U |   |
| P |   | E | A | S |   |
|   |   |   |   |   |   |
| R |   | M |   |   | Y |
|   |   |   |   |   |   |

*A* has already formed three words (and is after *teapot* and perhaps *safest*), *B* has two (and wants *queue*), and *C* has none so far (but with luck will get *please* and *fuss*). Altogether thirty-six letters are called and points can be given according to the number of words formed, or to those having the fewest squares occupied by letters not belonging to a word (these can be shaded in).

## Variants

*A* There are two, three, or four players. A class of twenty-eight learners would therefore be organized into at least seven groups. Each group has a board ruled into squares, and each player an identical set of letters (say thirty) small enough to be placed on these squares.

The game is to get rid of one's letters as soon as possible by forming nothing but words on the board. The first player begins with a whole word, and subsequently players must make their words by attaching letters to some part of the words on the board and not by placing them separately. Thus if the first player puts down RIVER in the middle of the board and the second player finds himself with F and two E's he can make FREE as in the diagram. The next player has L, I, and E, and can make LIVE, but only where it is shown and not next to FREE, because FL, EV and EE (which are not words) would result. Player 4 might possibly see nothing to do except add an S to RIVER.

|   |   |   | L |   |   |   |
|---|---|---|---|---|---|---|
|   | F | I |   |   |   |   |
|   | R | I | V | E | R | S |
|   | E | E |   |   |   |   |
|   | E |   |   |   |   |   |

*B* Each player has a square, as in 10.1 and 10.2, and each in his turn calls out a letter. The aim is to form words down and across with the letters given. The game should be kept going briskly, allowing about ten seconds between each letter. As soon as all the squares have been filled, the number of complete words is reckoned up. Five points are awarded for five-letter words, three for four-letter words, and one for others. Papers are exchanged for scrutiny and marking. Dictionaries are allowed. The teacher's spot check is essential.

10.2 *Collective scrabble*[1]. There is one big 'scrabble board' (set of squares) on the board, and some of the squares are numbered 2 and 3. A short word, such as TOMORROW, is printed in the middle. Groups (rather than teams) add words in turn: they can tell the teacher what to write in or the group leader can write it. All words added must of course be linked with a word already there.

If one of the letters of a word covers a square marked 2 or 3 the number of points for that word is doubled or trebled.

10.3 *Lotto* (see also Chapter 7.8, p. 123). At least one form of this game can give useful spelling practice when played in groups of three or four. Each player has a different word-card bearing three or four words of equal length, as shown below.

| P | E | N | C | I | L |
|---|---|---|---|---|---|
| E | N | G | I | N | E |
| B | O | T | T | L | E |
| M | A | R | K | E | T |

There is a pile of letter-cards face downwards on a table in the middle, and from these everybody takes one card in turn (alternatively, a box of letter-cards is passed round). If the letter a player takes does not appear in any of the words on his card, he returns it to the pile; if it does, he places it over that letter. The first to cover all the words on his card is the winner. Then the cards are exchanged and the next round of the game begins, but the players may write down the words on their cards before they exchange them. This is a fairly leisurely game.

## 11 Pattern puzzle

Level **intermediate and advanced**
Age **any**
Group size **groups, individuals**

Each group is given a card bearing a letter-pattern, the same on each, as in the example here. The players each write down on paper all the words they can think of containing some or all of these letters, provided that the middle letter (E in this example) appears in each one. No letter should be used more than once in any word. There is a time limit. The group with most words is the winner.

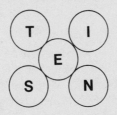

# 12 Crosswords

Level **intermediate and advanced**
Age **any (except young children)**
Group size **groups, individuals, whole class**

Simple ones are fairly easy to make, and come in useful year after year.

Various procedures are possible:

12.1 Everybody has the same crossword and solves it individually, with the help of the clues.

12.2 Each small group has a different crossword, and everyone in the group helps to solve it.

12.3 First of all, everybody works at the crossword individually, then they work in groups. This makes it more likely that every member of the group will contribute something.

12.4 There is a crossword on the board, but no written clues. Give these orally and solve the crossword step by step in conversation with the class. Learners come to the board and print the words in one by one, each team using differently coloured chalk. They can be written in on individual copies too. (*Word-squares* can also be played thus.)

Useful phrases (in English): *How many letters do we need?* (Referring to a clue) *Do you mean '6' down or '6' across? That's two letters too long/short. Does it end with ...?*

12.5 *Crossword relay.* There are two 'crossword' frames on the board (or more than two if there are more than two teams) consisting entirely of blank squares. Somebody says *Go* or *Begin* and a learner from each team hurries out, prints in one letter on the team crossword, and hands the chalk to the second person in the team, who adds another letter, and so on. All the members of each team do this, and try to build up words. Thus there must be enough squares – at least 16 if each team has 16 members. If there are more squares than members of the team, the first learner to go out continues writing in letters. Scoring is based on the number of letters in the words which appear. There can also be a time-limit, to encourage speed.

It is even better to have one 'crossword' for each group. If there are five learners in a group, there can still be, say 25 squares in the 'crossword', and each player will go out and add a letter five times. The advantage of basing the game on groups rather than relatively large teams is that it is easier for the members of a compact group to consult one another quickly on what to write in next.

# 13  Pictures

Level **elementary**
Age **children**
Group size **individuals and groups**

Collect especially (for spelling and reading games) pictures of objects, people, and activities the class has been talking about. Paste them on cards, leaving room underneath for a phrase or a short sentence.

Reading is chiefly a matter of reading whole words, phrases, and sentences (i.e. of understanding them in print), while spelling is chiefly a matter of writing letters in the usual order. Give the learners a stock of letter-cards and let them make words to suit the pictures. Under the picture of a house, for example, they should build up the phrase *a house* or *This is a house*, under a picture of a man or woman jumping either *jumping* or perhaps *John/Barbara is jumping*.

## Variant

If there are words already under the picture, they can be covered letter by letter with the letter-cards. A tray or box of letters is passed round the group, each taking one at a time (as for *Lotto* above) and putting back any letter which is unusable. Each learner has the same number of picture-cards. The first to cover all the words under his or her pictures (or to put suitable words there, correctly spelt) is the winner and scores a certain number of points; the next scores fewer points. The players can exchange their cards and start again.

## 14  Sentence relay

Level   **intermediate and advanced**
Age   **children**
Group size   **whole class**

At a leader's signal the first in each team runs to the board and writes a word, then back to his team, handing the chalk to the second player, who does likewise, and so on. The aim is to write a complete sentence, which must not come to an end until all the members of the team have written one word each. If a word is misspelt or illegible, it is rubbed out at once.

The words may be added either in front of or after what is already on the board.

See also page 137, game 5.

## 15  Spell aloud what you hear or know

Level   **intermediate and advanced**
Age   **any (except young children)**
Group size   **whole class, teams, groups**

Some of the spelling games already described are partly oral and can still be played if the written part is left out: for example, 1.4, 1.6, 2.3, and 6 in this chapter. 2.3 (*What's your word?*) is one of the simplest oral spelling games, but can be both useful and amusing. As for 2.5, challengers come in turn from different teams. If there are two teams, for example, each consisting of twenty learners, it is advisable to have at least twenty words. The first in Team A will say, perhaps, *Sailor, Jill*, and Jill, in Team B, will reply, *Sailor s-a-i-l-o-r*. She is right, and Team B scores a point. It is her turn now. *Soldier*, says Jill, looking at Team A., *Robert*. Robert answers uncertainly *S-o-l-d-a-r*. Poor Robert – no point for his team – a point for Team B instead! Jill asks somebody else in Team A, *Do you know, Violet?* Violet smiles. *S-o-l-d-i-e-r*. Good. A point for Team A. *What do soldiers do?* says the teacher, mindful of meaning. *Yes, they fight for their countries.* Violet's turn now. *Butcher, Audrey*. And so on.

15.1 *Finding the word*. There are a number of dots on the board, corresponding to the number of letters in a word not mentioned. Learners ask in turn questions such as *Has it an* a? *Is there a* t *in it? Does it contain a* g? (There is practice here in using two types of *yes/no* question.) If the answer is yes, the letter is written in where it occurs. If the answer is no, an *x* is put against the name of the team concerned. The team which has the fewest *x*s by the time the word is complete scores a point.

15.2 *Endbee*. One player gives the first letter of a word he has in mind, and the second player, who may be thinking of quite a different word, gives the second letter, and so on. The first one to complete a word of more than three letters is the winner.

## Variants

*A*   As above, except that the aim is to *avoid* completing a word at all. Thus if the first player says E, the second L, and the third M, we have ELM, and the third player is momentarily out. Back to EL now. If E is added, this might lead to ELECT or ELEPHANT, either of which would end the game.

Every player must have a word in mind as he supplies a letter, and can be challenged to say what it is.

*B*   As above, except that nobody has to drop out as a result of making a word, so long as letters can be added to make a longer word. For example, if ELECT is reached, there is still ELECTS or ELECTOR or ELECTION. Those drop out momentarily who complete a word which cannot be extended or who cannot extend one which can.

15.3 *Backs to the board*. There is a group of words on the board. Everybody studies these, and then one or two from each team come out and face the class. They are then challenged by others in the class to spell various words on the board. As soon as all the words have been given twice, those in front sit down and others take their places. Anybody making a mistake has also to sit down, and is replaced by another member of his team. A team point can be given for every correct spelling.

15.4 *Thinking of words*. This can be played within groups or between groups or teams. Here is an example.

John: *Can you think of an animal whose name begins with* C? Molly: *Yes.* John: *What is it?* Molly: *A camel.* John: *Spell it.* Molly: *C-a-m-e-l.* John: *Right.* Molly wins a point for her team. If John says it is not right, she gets two. If he fails to notice an error, his team does not score.

Molly (continuing): *Tell me the name of a plant ending with s.* Bill (in John's team): *Cactus.* Molly: *Spell it.* Bill: *C-a-c-t-u-s.* And so on, using familiar words.

Vary the wording if the class is advanced enough. *Give/Tell me the name of . . . Can you tell me . . . ? Can you think of . . . ?* etc.

15.5  *Likes and dislikes.* A full description of this game is given in Chapter 10.6, p. 176. As is evident from some of the samples there, it is readily adaptable to spelling practice. The puzzling statements about George (or whoever it is) can, for instance, be *He likes bread but he doesn't like beans/likes peas but not cabbage/likes pears but not apples,* focusing attention in due course on words spelt with *ea.* Further examples . . . likes *photographs* but not *films, telephoning* but not *flying* (representation of /f/as *ph* or *f* ); *monkeys* but not *donkeys, money* but not *dollars,* etc. (*o* representing/ʌ/), and so on.

Some classes may find this difficult to begin with, and it will doubtless be necessary to write the sentences (or certain words) on the board before the point is grasped.

This is not a game that can be played often.

## Notes and references

1 See 'Scrabble – with variations' by Helen Moorwood in *Modern English Teacher*, Volume 4, Number 2, 1976, p. 12.

# Chapter 4
# PRONUNCIATION GAMES

Errors made in pronouncing a foreign language vary to a certain extent from one mother tongue to another, although some are widespread. Listening and speaking habits formed during the process of acquiring the mother tongue make it hard for the learners to hear and make differences of sound which are unimportant in that mother tongue. In such circumstances it is no good asking impatiently Can't you hear what I am saying? Yet it can be helpful to isolate the sound and point out visible features of its formation, such as the position of the jaws and lips. Indeed, this in itself may enable learners to hear it better. Until they can hear that there is a difference between what they say and what they should say, there will not be much advance.

Pronunciation drills, which can take the form of games or contests, should be held regularly, but not for long periods; five minutes every lesson may be enough, with a longer stretch occasionally. They should be as meaningful as possible. Although it is necessary to isolate sounds from time to time, sentence examples such as The man outside ran away and The men outside ran away do help learners to realize that what may seem a very small difference of sound can accompany a big difference of meaning. But at an elementary stage, while the learners' vocabulary is very small, these drills and games may have to be based on isolated words and sounds.

The games, contests, and activities which follow are, of course, merely illustrative. The pronunciation difficulties reflected in the examples given are not met with everywhere. Adaptation to local problems is necessary.

Learners can act as the teacher in these activities but should not do so unless their pronunciation is reasonably good. The teacher tells the learner what to say or writes it on a piece of paper. If it is spoken accurately the learner's team can win a point, apart from any points others may win with their answers. It is interesting that inability to make their fellow learners understand what they are saying does a lot to convince learners of the shortcomings of their own pronunciation. Note: As the games and activities which follow are all meant to help pronunciation, the use of the games will not be stated.

69

# 1 The same or different

Level **elementary and intermediate**
Age **any (except younger children)**
Group size **whole class**

This game can be played with sounds, words, or sentences. It goes roughly as follows:

The teacher says two sentences and the learners decide whether they are the same or different. Examples:

Teacher: *'We began to think.*
*We began to sink.'*
*Are they the same? I'll say them*
*once more . . . Peter?*
Peter: *The second one was different.*
Teacher: *Right. Listen again:*
*'That's a good road.*
*That's a good road.'*
John: *Different.*
Teacher: *Listen again.* (Repeats them)
John: *The same.*
Teacher: *Yes, now listen again.*
*'I'd like to look at your bag.*
*I'd like to look at your back.'*
*Hands up.*

And so on. Sometimes the sentences are given in pairs, sometimes in threes or fours, and often they will be identical, often different. The teacher should sometimes say *Listen again* even when the answer is right.

It is essential that each sentence of a pair should be spoken in exactly the same way (e.g. with the same stress and intonation) apart from the one difference between them.

## Variants

*A* As above, except that minimal pairs are used. Examples: *leaf-leave men-men-man thick-sick-sick Mary-merry-Mary ride-hide-hide*, etc.

*B* Two or more words or syllables are pronounced and the class must say whether they rhyme or not. Example: *bad, mad, bed, sad* – oral answer *'No'* to the third one – written answer 1-2-4, or (if only the odd word is to be noted) 3. If the answers are written, S can be used for 'same' and D for 'different'.

C   As under A, except that isolated sounds are used, e.g. /e/ and /æ/, or /θ/, /s/, and /t/. Alternatively the sounds can be presented in syllables.

D   Material similar to that mentioned above can be recorded beforehand on tape and played to the class. This can be an advantage when the teacher's own pronunciation is not very good, but also when it is – as a means of bringing in a man's voice, for instance, when the teacher is a woman, or a woman's voice when the teacher is a man. The recordings should have been made by speakers of English using the type of pronunciation which is aimed at in the country concerned. A key must be available to the teacher. The exercises can be played as under the above headings, except that the material is heard from a tape recorder, stopped after each set of examples has been given. If there are several repetitions of each set of examples, it may not be necessary to stop the tape. Written answers are preferable to oral ones when a tape recording is used.

Stress and intonation difficulties can be dealt with similarly, although most *children*, at least, seem to pick up their teacher's stress and intonation (whether appropriate or inappropriate) very readily, and run into difficulty only with 'sounds' (in the narrow sense) and sequences of 'sounds'.

It is the *meaning* of the sentence or longer stretch of language, within the whole context of what is being said and what is and has been going on, that decides what stress and intonation should be used. Nevertheless it is helpful, if learners persistently use stress or intonation patterns inappropriate to the meaning, to present the 'right' one and the 'wrong' one (in the particular context) in contrast, for until the learner can be got to *hear* that there is a difference between the two, he will continue to follow his accustomed usage.

As far as stress patterns are concerned, the learner's difficulty is often one of *placing* the strong stresses. Practise sentences differing in stress placement, but in such a way that the different placements of the stress accompany definable differences of meaning. This may help adult learners in particular.

Examples
**She** *was carrying a red umbrella.* (Not somebody else.)
*She* **was** *carrying a red umbrella.* (You're wrong to suggest she wasn't.)
*She was* **carrying** *a red umbrella.* (She was carrying it, not holding it up.)
*She was carrying a* **red** *umbrella.* (Not a green one.)
*She was carrying a red* **umbrella.** (Not a red coat.)

As a general rule, only teachers with training in phonetics can be sure of the intonation pattern they are using in a particular utterance and can produce particular intonation patterns at will.

## 2  Which is which?

> Level  **elementary, intermediate, and advanced**
> Age  **any (except younger children)**
> Group size  **whole class**

These drill-games are like those described under 1, but more is expected of the learners. They do not simply have to decide whether the utterances are different or the same, but to identify them.

The presentation can be oral or both oral and visual.

Suppose the pupils can hear there is a difference between /i/ and /ɪ/ as in *'You must leave there'* and *'You must live there.'* *Let's call 'leave'* (go away) *A,* says the teacher, *and 'live'* (live in a place) *B. Now, listen. Which is this? 'You must live there'. Tom? Mary? Yes, it's B. Now what about this?* And so on, with scoring of team points if necessary.

Learners can take the teacher's place if they are good enough, but must be supervised.

Responses can be either oral or written. If the response is written, pupils write A or B or the words themselves.

For the sake of fun and to keep the class alert, introduce occasionally a sound which is neither of the two, even if the word in which it is put is non-existent, as in *You must /lev/ there. Neither* is the only acceptable response.

If isolated words are being used, several can be given at once, the class being told, for instance, *Write A if you hear the vowel sound of 'bed'* (the thing you sleep in) *and B if you hear the vowel* sound of *'bad'* (the opposite of good). Now – *'set, set, sat, set.'* The answer should be A,A,B,A.

## Variants

*A*   There is a set of words on the blackboard, e.g. *part, pot, port*. These are lettered or numbered in some way, e.g. as A, B, and C. The teacher says, for example, *not*, and expects the answer B.

It is more interesting to have several sets of known words on the board at the same time. Thus for discrimination among /f/, /θ/, /s/, and /t/ there might be the following:

| A | fin | four | half | fight |
|---|-----|------|------|-------|
| B | thin | thaw | hearth | – |
| C | sin | saw | – | sight |
| D | tin | taw | heart | tight |

As a word is pronounced, pupils have to say what line it is in.

If a class is familiar with phonetic symbols, they can be used in these games.

*B*   Similarly with stress and intonation. A stress example might be shown thus:

1   *Don't telephone ME tomorrow* (but you can ring somebody else.)
2   *Don't TELephone me tomorrow* (you can write, perhaps.)
3   *DON'T telephone me tomorrow* (I didn't say 'Telephone me' but 'Don't telephone me.')

Here the italics show stressed syllables and block capitals the main stresses.

Intonation examples are most easily grasped if the line of print follows the rises and falls of the voice, as in:

A.   What did $^{y}o_{u}$ say?

B.   What $d_{i}{}_{d}$ you say?

C.   What $did$ $^{you}$ $^{say?}$

# 3 Pronunciation bingo

Level **intermediate**
Age **any (except young children)**
Group size **whole class**

This game is similar to other *Bingo* games, except that the focus of attention is on how something is pronounced.

Every member of the class has a card bearing a number of pictures, say six, and a larger number of separate pictures, each of the same size. What pictures these are should depend mainly on what the pronunciation difficulties are in the learners' country. If, for instance, discrimination of /θ/ from /s/ is not one of the difficulties, there would be little point in including pictures of a mouth and a mouse, whereas a pot and a port might be very relevant.

The cards are not identical. Each one has on it only some of all the pictures in use. The separate pictures which each player also has may include some which are not on his card. The cards and separate pictures are distributed at random.

The teacher calls out a series of words, corresponding with what is in the pictures, and the players look at their cards and their loose pictures to see whether they have what is called. Thus if *a ship* is called they will look for pictures of a ship (or, mistakenly, of a sheep), and if they have them both on the card and separately they will cover the one on the card with the loose picture.

The first to have all the pictures on their cards covered raise their hands.

## Variants

*A* Instead of pictures on the cards, there can be words. The 'caller' does not say these words, of which he has a complete list, but words that rhyme with them. For example, if the list contains *bed*, *bad*, *sit*, *seat*, *hut*, and *heart* he says words such as *head*, *had*, *bit*, *feet*, *nut*, and *part*. The players cross off on their cards any word which rhymes with the word called.

*B* As for A, except that the player listens for the initial consonant and crosses off only those words on the card which seem to have the same one. Thus if *hole* is called, the listener can cross off *hall* or *heap* but not *roll*; if *thick* is called, *thin* or *thief* can be crossed off, and so on.

# 4 Are you saying it?

Level **intermediate**
Age **any (except young children)**
Group size **whole class, teams, groups**

It is not enough to be able to recognize differences between speech sounds; one must also be able to produce them. Production exercises can also take the form of games. For instance:

As a means of overcoming persistent difficulties with the pronunciation of sounds, a team contest may be arranged. Suppose the difficulty is poor discrimination between /v/ as in *veal* and /w/ as in *wheel*. Assuming that the formation of these sounds, in particular the lip positions, has been demonstrated, one team can take /v/-words and the other /w/-words, and then change. To begin with, a few members of each team are called upon to say one or the other kind of word (these will be on the board or can be given orally). Then small groups within each team can be given a minute or two to find two-word or three-word phrases containing both /v/-words and /w/-words. Points are awarded for the way in which they say these, and the opposite team can be involved in the adjudication.

Possible phrases: *very wet/very warm, worse verses, wet violets*.

# 5 What are you saying?

Level **intermediate**
Age **any (except young children)**
Group size **whole class**

There are some numbered sentences on the board which differ slightly from one another in pronunciation but greatly in meaning. Examples:

1a *I can't find my class.*
 b *I can't find my glass.*
2a *Ballet-dancers work very hard.*
 b *Belly-dancers work very hard.*
3a *The trees are full of birds.*
 b *The trees are full of buds.*
4a *We shall leave there.*
 b *We shall live there.*[1]

Students take it in turn to read any sentence aloud (there should be about twenty on the board, based on the learners' actual difficulties with sounds) and various members of the same team mention the number of the sentence they think has been read.

# 6 Pictures and sounds

Level **elementary**
Age **any**
Group size **whole class**

Pictures are useful for a variety of purposes in the foreign language course, and some pronunciation difficulties lend themselves to pictorial illustration. For instance, there can be simple pictures of a pot and a port, a sheep and a ship, a hat and a hut, a cart and a kite, a rope and a robe, a hat and a rat, somebody thinking and somebody sinking, a fairy and a ferry, and so on. Here are some such sketches.

Although they can be quickly drawn on the board, it is preferable to have such pictures on cards which can be kept, since they provide useful test material as well as practice material. Be sure that the sketches are big enough and clear enough to be seen properly from the back of the class.

Pronunciation games or contests can be played with pictures of this sort as follows. (Here the pictures of a hut and a hat are taken as examples.)

6.1 The pictures are numbered 1 and 2. The teacher asks *Which is the hat?* (i.e. which of the two?) or *Which is the hut?* Hands go up, and answers (1 or 2) are taken from several learners in each team, those who are right scoring a point. (Other pictures similarly).

## Variants

*A* As above, except that answers are written. Several sets of pictures are used. The teacher keeps a record of what he says, and correction should be made immediately afterwards, not merely by reading out the right answers but by giving the examples again as well. Papers can be exchanged between teams.

*B* The teacher asks *Which is the hat/hut?* or says *Point to the hat/hut*, and then names someone (from each team in turn) who goes to the board and points or says *This is the hat/hut. Is he /she right?* the teacher asks. No score if the learner is wrong.

*C* Pointing to one of the pictures, the teacher asks, *Is this a ...?* naming someone or several people to answer. Or the teacher may use question tags, e.g. *This is a ..., isn't it?*, or an alternative question, e.g. *Is this a ... or a ...?* The learner should be taught to ask similar questions of one another.

*D* The teacher says *Draw a hat* or *Draw a hut*. Everybody draws on paper what they think has been said, and some of course draw the wrong thing. The papers are exchanged and a tick is put against correct drawings, a cross against incorrect ones. A point is scored for every correct drawing. (Drawing skill is unnecessary, so long as a hat, for example, looks different from a hut.)

*E* As for D, except that two or more learners from different teams draw on the board at the same time. This version of the game should not be played unless the pupils can sketch well enough and *quickly* enough.

6.2 If learners have their own picture-cards, other games can be played. For example, the teacher says *Show me a hat*. Those who hold up a *hat* card at once win a team point. Extra scorers may be needed.

## Variants

*A* The teacher says, for instance, *Change huts*, and everybody should hand over a *hut* card to somebody in another team. All then hold up the cards they have. Those who know they have been given a wrong card (i.e. in this instance, one of a hat) will be eager to call attention to it, so that a rival team gains fewer points; they can hold such a card upside down. Those who do not know they have a wrong card will not do this and will thus not contribute to the score (which is the number of members of the rival team minus the number of cards held upside down). During this game learners should be discouraged from looking about at each other's cards, apart from those they exchange: it is listening that matters.

B   The learners are in groups, each of which has a pile of cards on a desk or table. The piles are exactly the same for each group, and each contains several copies (say 4) of each picture: if there are six different pictures, there will thus be 24 cards in a pile. This should be enough for a group of four or five. The teacher says, for instance, *Find a hat*, and the first group to hold up all four *hat* cards gets a point (or a point for the team it belongs to).

C   Cards are hidden in various parts of the room. The class is told what to look for, and the team or group with most cards of the right kind at the end of, say, two minutes gets a point. This game can be played only where there is room to move about and the class is a fairly small one. Whispering is discouraged. Variety can be given by including real objects as well; finding one counts for as much as finding a picture of one.

*Note:* Pictures need not be presented in twos; there may be a larger number in the set. For instance, a picture of a *heart* may be added to those of a *hut* and a *hat*, and of a *cot* or *cat* to those of a *cart* or *kite*. It depends on what practice in discriminating between sounds is required, and also to a large extent on what can be done within the limits of vocabulary so far acquired. If they contain what is needed, pictures of scenes may be used in the same way as pictures of separate objects or actions.

Learners' cards need not be so big as those used by the teacher for the whole class. They should not be so small, however, that the teacher cannot see from a distance what they are.

## 7   Say what you mean

|            |                              |
|-----------:|------------------------------|
| Level      | **intermediate and advanced** |
| Age        | **any**                      |
| Group size | **whole class**              |

Here is a type of pronunciation game in which there is a very close link between sounds and meaning.

The teacher says, for instance, *What do people sometimes wear on their heads? Hats. Right. Do they wear huts on their heads? Of course not. But some people live in huts. Where? Does anyone live in a hat?* (There could be matchstick figures on the board of somebody wearing a hat and somebody sitting at the door of a hut, as well as ridiculous ones of somebody with a hut on his head and somebody sitting on a hat.) *Now, listen. Tell me whether I am right or wrong. Some people live in hats ... Some people live in huts ... Some of us wear huts ...* and so on. Write R for *right* and W for *wrong*.

## Variants

*A* The teacher says *Draw a hut/hat*, etc. The learners, without looking at each other's papers, draw quickly what they think has been asked for. Similarly *cup/cap, pot/port, ball/bowl, boot/boat, bird/bud, coat/goat, hole/roll, pens/pence, mouth/mouse*. This is not suitable for learners (and teachers) who do not enjoy making quick rough amusing sketches.[2]

*B* There are possibilities in physical action, if miming is included and the ridiculous is not excluded, e.g. *Fill/Feel my pocket. Give me a pen/pin. Watch/Wash the door.*

Ingenuity is called for in finding contexts of use for sentences containing sounds which need to be practised.

# 8 Speaking at length

| | |
|---|---|
| Level | **intermediate** |
| Age | **children** |
| Group size | **whole class or teams** |
| Use | **intonation practice (surprise questions and short assertions)** |

8.1 *Mr Roy's Watch.* This game gives practice in certain intonation patterns. It is sometimes called *The Prince of Wales's hat.*

The players, who could be sitting or standing in a circle, are first given numbers. The teacher begins: *Mr Roy has lost his watch and No.[3] 6 has found it.*

Appropriate intonations are graphically suggested in the diagram below. If the learners are familiar with each other's names, these can be used instead of numbers. The game need not be competitive, although it can easily be played between two teams, if the next learner named is always opposite one.

No.6: Who? Me, Mr Smith?

Teacher: Yes, you, No.6.

No.6: Not me, Mr Smith.

Teacher: Then who, No.6?

No.6: Number twelve, Mr Smith.

No.12: Who? Me, No.6?

No.6: Yes, you, No.12.

No.12: Not me, No.6.

No.6: Then who, No.12?

No.12: Number eight, No.6.

Level   **intermediate and advanced**
Age   **any (except young children)**
Group size   **whole class and teams**

8.2 *Spoken Messages*. The difficulty of passing a spoken message unchanged from one learner to another along a line or round a circle helps to bring home the importance of clear intelligible speech. This is a game most easily played outdoors or where there is plenty of room so that the players can be well spaced out. The teacher gives the message orally to the team leaders and at the word *Go* they whisper it to the next member of the team, who whispers it to No. 3, and so on. The last member of each team to receive the whispered message either says it aloud or, perhaps better, writes it down for the teacher (or other originator of the message) to read out. The team which has managed to pass the message through with least change gains a point.

Messages must be neither too easy nor too difficult, and should be interesting for the age of the learners concerned. They should also contain some of the pronunciation difficulties with which they have been struggling. Probably the most suitable type of message is a command, which the last player has to obey. Examples: *Say three times 'I shall live with Tom's brother and mother'. Walk once round the table and twice round the teacher and then sit down. Draw a sheep and a boat at the side of the board.*

# 9  Likes and dislikes

Level **intermediate and advanced**
Age **any (except young children)**
Group size **whole class**

See Chapter 10.6, p. 176. This game can be adapted so that the ultimate focus of attention is a pronunciation point. Examples:
*X likes watches but he doesn't like clocks; wheels but not bicycles or cars; windows but not doors; twilight but not dawn or dusk* (i.e. he likes words containing /w/). *Y likes veal but he doesn't like meat; violets but not flowers; virtue but not goodness; volcanoes but not lava; lovers but not sweethearts* (i.e. he likes words containing /v/).

There is a semantic link between what is liked and what is disliked, and the listener's attention first focuses on the meaning, which is puzzling. For example, how is it possible that somebody can like wheels but not a bicycle?

This is the sort of game that cannot be played many times, perhaps only once within its field of reference (here pronunciation).

If the two sounds concerned are both included in the statement, the 'solution' will be found very quickly and the resulting 'impact' on the learner will be weaker. Examples: *X likes wheels but he doesn't like veal; watches but not violins.* This is also more inconsequential, as the semantic link between the two items is not close.

# 10 Suggestions for dealing with particular faults

Here are some exercises, some of them rather like games, which can help overcome various widespread difficulties with the pronunciation of English.

**a** *Fault:* Insufficient aspiration (i.e. breathiness) of the English /p/, /t/, and /k/ sounds occurring at the beginning of stressed syllables.

*Exercises*

i) Strike a match and hold the flame near your lips. Then say *puff* or *park* or some other words beginning with a /p/ sound. The flame should go out at once. If it does not, insufficient aspiration has been used. (*NB.* Aspirated /t/ and /k/ may make the flame only wobble.)

ii) Hold up a small piece of very thin paper near the lips and say *pet, take, Kate,* etc. If the paper is not blown back a little like a flag fluttering in the breeze, the aspiration is insufficient.

iii) Put the lips lightly together and pretend to be blowing out a candle. Then add a /p/ sound lazily before this. Reduce the breathiness.

**b** *Fault:* Substitution of a fricative for a stop sound, especially between vowels, as in *rubber* and *ladder*. (To an English ear there then seems to be a /v/ sound or a /ð/ sound, as in *this*, in the middle of these words.)

*Exercise*

For a /b/ sound press the lips firmly together, holding the breath, and try to make a small 'explosion' in the middle of such words – *ruBBer, haBit, roBin, riBBon*. Then try to get the same feeling and effect with /d/ and /g/ sounds, as in *laDDer, hiDing, biGGer, foGGy, reaDing*.

**c** *Fault:* Too little difference between /v/ and /w/ sounds.

*Exercise*

For /v/, bite your bottom lip. Now blow and say ffff. Now sing it, vvvv. Sing 'London Bridge', or some other well-known tune, with the sound /v/ (not və). Keep on biting your bottom lip.

For /w/, say *moon*, and then prolong the *oo* sound with your lips rounded like the full moon. Now say *oowee* (we), *ooway* (way),

83

*oowI* (why), *ooair* (where) etc. The lip rounding for /w/ can also be obtained by rounding the lips as for whistling.

**d** *Fault:* Failure to make the /θ/ and /ð/ sounds as in *thief* and *this* properly.
*Exercise*
Put out your tongues; the doctor wants to see them. Now blow. Tell the doctor, with your tongue out: *I'm thick.* Now put your tongues back inside and say *I'm sick.*

**e** *Fault:* Failure to make the /ʃ/ as in *ship* well.
*Exercise*
Pretend to be a railway engine (steam) pulling out a train from the station, slowly at first, then more quickly: sh - sh - sh- sh-sh-sh-sh . . . Push out your lips well and round them too.

**f** *Fault:* Failure to make an /s/ sound well.
*Exercise*
Try hissing like an angry snake. If the sound is too 'sharp', try the effect of rounding the lips a little.

**g** *Fault:* Failure to make the sound /h/– substitution (often) of the sound at the end of the Scottish word *loch*, so that *hole* and *roll* are not well discriminated.
*Exercise*
Panting. Pretend that you have been running to catch a bus or train. You are out of breath, and produce a series of excellent /h/ sounds as you pant to recover it.

**h** *Fault:* Failure to make the /tʃ/ sound as in *church* properly.
*Exercise*
Pretend to be a railway engine – a slightly different kind from that in **e**. (Imitation of the teacher.)

**i** *Fault:* Failure to pronounce the /ð/ sound as in *this*, the /v/ and /z/ sounds and the sound in the middle of *pleasure*, with sufficient 'buzz' (vibration, 'voice').
*Exercise*
Start from the corresponding /θ/ sound in *thief* (see **d** above) or from /f/ or /s/ or /ʃ/, and try to sing them. For /z/, imitate the buzzing of angry bees. The buzzing can be felt if you touch the lump in your throat under your chin.

**j** *Fault:* Failure to stress common types of utterance in an appropriate way.

*Exercises*

i) Tapping on the desk, or nodding the head, in time with the strong beats of the sentence, as in:

> *When* are you *go*ing to *read* it *again*?
> I *wasn't* the *first* to *no*tice it.
> On the *other side* of the *street* was a *ci*nema.
> The *story ends* on *page three*.
> They *packed* their be*long*ings in an *old suit*case.
> etc.

ii) Tapping the rhythm and 'hearing' the sentence silently.

iii) Tapping the rhythm and making up sentences to fit it. (*NB*. If there are several weakly stressed syllables between the strong beats, there is a tendency to speak them more quickly, in order to keep the regularity of the rhythm. This does not mean that the strongly stressed syllables occur at equal intervals of time: adjacent strong stresses, for example, slow down the speed of that part of the sentence.)

iv) Somebody taps out the rhythm of one of the practice sentences; others guess which sentence has been tapped.

v) Tapping the rhythm of a sentence or phrase first, and then saying it at the same speed in the same way.

**k.** *Fault:* Failure to use a suitable intonation pattern.

*Exercise*

Slowing utterances down and drawling them out (so long as the intonation pattern is kept the same), and exaggerated hand and arm movements indicating the upward and downward movement, the hills and the valleys of pitch, can often enable learners to hear and grasp the pattern, however absurd the exaggeration may be.

## Notes and references

1 Numerous examples will be found in *Drills and Tests in English Sounds* by L. A. Hill.

2 See *English Pronunciation Illustrated* by John Trim.

3 An abbreviation for *Number* and pronounced the same way.

# Chapter 5
# NUMBER GAMES

*Many games help the learner to get accustomed to the spoken forms of numbers, so that they are not a stumbling block to communication. Here are a few of these. Although they are oral games, in some there can be reading and writing as well.*

*All the games that follow help to familiarize the learners with the spoken form of numbers.*

## 1 Ring a number

Level **elementary and intermediate**
Age **children**
Group size **whole class, teams**

Various numbers are written clearly and firmly on the board, in a group, something like this:

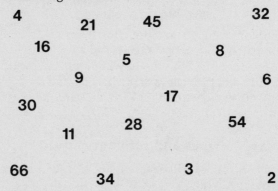

They need not be 1–20; indeed, if everybody is already confidently using such numbers in speech, they should be other numbers, with which they are not yet confident. They should all be written at a height the learners can reach.

There are two teams and one member from each stands at the board, coloured chalk in hand (each team has a different colour).

Somebody stands at the side and calls out one of the numbers. Immediately the two look for it, and the first to put a ring round it scores a point.

Those out at the board should be replaced by the next in the teams after, say, three numbers have been called.

This game usually arouses great interest and excitement.

In place of numbers, there can be clock times, weights and measures, dates, sums of money, telephone numbers, etc.

## Variants

*A*   It is possible to play this game as a kind of relay race. The teams are lined up at right angles to the board and facing it, but behind a chalk-line. When the first number is called, the first in each team rushes forward and tries to be the first to put a ring round it. They then go to the back of their teams but on the way hand the chalk to the next in the team, who compete to ring the second word called. And so on. There should be more numbers on the board than members of one team. Points are scored as above.

*B*   Instead of one set of numbers on the board, there are two (or more than two if there are more than two teams). The words are successively called as soon as a member of *one* team has ringed the previous one. Each team uses its own part of the board. The winning team is the first one to have crossed out all the numbers called.

*C*   As for A and B, except that the teams have their backs to the board. After ringing a number, each player goes back to his or her seat.

If a mistake is made, the teacher corrects it as quickly as possible, but this of course delays the team. Alternatively, the one who has made the mistake corrects it by rubbing out, re-writing, and encircling the number.

# 2  How many?

|  |  |
|---|---|
| Level | **elementary** |
| Age | **younger children** |
| Group size | **whole class, teams** |

This is rather obvious but can also be fun. Somebody claps a number of times, or taps on a desk or table, or on the board, and then asks *How many?*

Similarly the class can be told to clap or tap a certain number of times together, or learners from different teams at the board can be told to make a certain number of circles or stars or crosses (and the quickest is the winner).

These are ways of familiarizing young children with the smaller numbers in the foreign language. The different activities can be mixed, especially when the class is taken as a whole; for instance: *clap three times – now tap four times on your desks; clap twice – tap five times*, etc.

Clapping, tapping, etc. can help the class to feel the meaning of certain common adverbs, e.g. *Clap loudly/softly/quickly/slowly*. There is also a situation here for the use of comparative forms: *Clap more loudly/less loudly. Don't clap so loudly. Tap more quickly than John/as loudly as Mary/twice as quickly as Peter*, etc. What does it all mean? They find out by doing it.

# 3 Guess how many

Level **elementary**
Age **children**
Group size **pairs and groups**

The learners work in pairs. Each has a small number of beans or marbles (or whatever object is convenient) and takes turns with his or her partner to guess how many there are in the other's closed hand. The pair can keep their own score – a point, say, every time a correct guess is made.

## Variants

*A* Guessing the weight or height of various learners can, if some means of weighing or measuring is available, involve also the use of comparatives and superlatives (*taller than, not so tall as, shorter than, as heavy as, heavier than, the heaviest*, etc.) Competitions in guessing the weight, length, height, or size of an object such as a ball, a cake, a doll, a chair, a street, a piece of string or ribbon, a box of chocolates, a field, or a building are easy to arrange.

*B   Odd or even:* A holds out his closed hand and asks *'odd or even?'*[1] B guesses one or the other, A opens his hand, and they count the objects aloud together. Then they change roles.

## 4  Team arithmetic

Level **elementary**
Age **any**
Group size **whole class, teams**

Brief spells of arithmetical cross-questioning between teams also help to make numbers in the foreign language more familiar. No. 1 in Team A says, for instance, *What are seven and four?*, waits a moment or two, and then chooses somebody in Team B to answer, e.g. Alice. Alice says *eleven*, and then asks someone in Team A *What's three times five?* If anyone gives a wrong answer, the opposite team calls attention to it and gets an extra turn; otherwise, the teacher points out the mistake.

Arithmetically the game should not be made difficult – it is language practice rather than practice in arithmetical thinking.

## 5  Number bingo

Level **elementary and intermediate**
Age **any**
Group size **groups or a small class**

Each member of the group has a card bearing numbers, as shown here:

| 13 | 1 | 4 | 30 | 28 | 19 | 6 |
|----|---|---|----|----|----|---|
| 2 | 5 | 21 | 17 | 25 | 14 | 9 |

Every card is different and no number appears twice. The leader has a checking table (a card or sheet on which appear all the numbers on the cards) and a set of counters (cardboard discs or squares, each about the same size as the squares on the cards).

If the numbers run from, say, 1 to 30, there will be 30 of these counters. The leader picks them up in any order and calls out the number on each one.

Suppose the leader calls *17*. Whoever has 17 on his or her card says *Yes* and covers it with 17 counter. The next number called may be *4*, which will be taken by someone else who has a card which includes 4.

The winner is the first to have all the numbers on a card covered.

Instead of straightforward numbers, the cards could of course be fractions (e.g. ¾, ⅓, 2⅕), decimals (e.g. 2.5, 3.7, .001)[2], weights and measures (e.g. 1 lb 2 ozs, 2½ kgs)[3], clock times (e.g. 3.30, 9.41, 10.59, 2.10)[4], etc.

## 6  Missing numbers

Level **elementary**
Age **children**
Group size **whole class, teams, groups**

The learners say the numbers (from a given starting point) as far as they can go, but instead of saying, for instance, 5, they clap their hands, tap on the desk, twiddle their thumbs, or say *Buzz*. They do the same with multiples of the number concerned – if it is 5, for example, they miss 10, 15, or 20.

They may also say the numbers in turn instead of in chorus. The learners who are the 'missing numbers' say nothing, but instead perform the action agreed on.

Those who make a mistake are 'out'. In a small class they will soon be 'in' again, if the game is played more than once, but in a large class they will be 'out' for a longer time. However, to mitigate the effect of this, everybody can have two 'lives' and will be out only if they make a mistake twice.

# 7 Peter is calling Paul

Level **elementary**
Age **children**
Group size **small class, or groups of about 12**

The learners form a circle in which Peter is next to Paul and the others each have numbers. The game begins with Peter saying, *Peter is calling Paul.* Paul replies by calling any one of the others, and says, for instance, *Paul is calling nine.* No. 9 must then respond without hesitation and call someone else, e.g. *Nine is calling eleven.* So it continues, with each one called immediately calling another. Anybody failing to respond immediately goes to stand next to the one with the highest number. All the players then 'number off' again, and some find themselves with new numbers.

Peter and Paul can be called too. If they do not respond at once they go to the place, and everybody moves up one, there is a new Peter and Paul, and everybody re-numbers.

The numbers need not begin from one, but from some higher number, e.g. 12 or 20. The game can also be played with ordinals and clock times, e.g. *The eighth is calling the fourteenth. Two o'clock is calling a quarter past seven.*

# 8 Number change

Level **elementary**
Age **children**
Group size **small class, or groups of 10 to 12**

The learners stand or sit in a circle and number off, e.g. *I'm number ten, Sue Nelson. I'm number twelve, Martin Brown*, etc. In the centre there is somebody who calls out any two numbers (but none higher than the numbers taken by those in the circle). If he calls out 3 and 8, for instance, 3 and 8 quickly change places. At the same time he must try to occupy one of their vacant places. If he succeeds, the player who now has no place in the circle goes to the centre and calls numbers.

# 9 Number snatch

Level **elementary**
Age **children**
Group size **teams**

Two teams of numbered players line up opposite each other.
Either No. 1 faces No. 1, No. 2 No. 2, etc. or (assuming, for
instance, that there are 30 players) No. 1 faces No. 15, No. 2
No. 14, etc. The numbers need not begin at 1.

There is a stool half-way between the two teams, and on it an
object which can easily be picked up, e.g. a ball, a nut, or a duster
(nothing which tears easily).

A number is called out – for instance, *eleven*. No. 11 in both
teams runs to the centre and tries to snatch the object and take it
back without being touched by his or her opponent. Success is
rewarded with a team point. The object is now replaced and
another number called. Everybody has at least one turn. The
team winning most points is the winner.

# 10 Catching

Level **elementary**
Age **young children**
Group size **teams or groups**

Each member of the group or team has a number. The leader
throws a ball into the air or up against a wall, and calls one of
these numbers. The one whose number this is runs forward to
try to catch the ball before it bounces. Doing so earns two points,
catching it after it bounces one point.

## 11  The man in the moon

Level **elementary**
Age **children**
Group size **whole class, teams, groups**

The learners stand or sit in a ring and number off, not necessarily from 1. Somebody in the centre says very clearly:

*The man in the moon has lost his hat.*
*Some say this and some say that,*
*But I say* (slight pause and then quickly)
*That number . . . has it.*

Everybody then counts aloud together up to the number mentioned: *One-two-three-four,* etc. No. 7 says *I haven't got it.* The one in the centre asks: *Who has it, then?* No. 7: *Number three has.* Everybody: *One-two-three.* No. 3: *No, I haven't got it.* And so on, until every player has been accused. The conclusion can be:

*The man in the moon,* etc.
*And* I *say*
*That nobody has it.*

Everybody then counts aloud from 1 to 20 (or whatever the number of players is).

Another phrase may, of course, be substituted for 'the man in the moon', e.g. *The witch in the forest, The old man in the village.*

## 12  What's the time now?

Level **elementary**
Age **children**
Group size **whole class, teams, groups**

'What's the time' now is one simple and obvious game, the hands being set and re-set in various positions: this can be done by various learners, with teams alternating. Also: *Show me . . .* (naming various times, *a quarter past three, eight o'clock, half past two, ten thirty,* etc.) Both can easily be played as a team competition.

If those who set the hands do so without letting others see, a guessing game can be played: *It's half past eight.* (*No, guess again*). *It's a quarter to nine.* (*No, it isn't a quarter to nine*). *It's twenty-three minutes to two.* (*No*), etc. This game can be played in pairs and in groups.

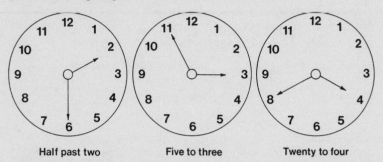

| Half past two | Five to three | Twenty to four |

A model clock is very useful. The numerals on it should not, at our elementary stage, be Roman (I, II, III, etc.) but Arabic (1, 2, 3, etc.) and they should all be upright as in the diagrams below, so that they are easily read. The hands should be easy to manipulate from the back of the clock-face.

A model clock may show not only the hours but the minutes as in the diagrams below. If the learners are so young that telling the time is new to them in any language, this type of model clock is preferable to begin with, because the learners then have in front of them confirmation of what they must say: e.g. for *twenty to four* they can see *20* and not merely *8*. The words *a quarter* and *half*, and the figures which indicate the minutes, can be shown in a different colour from those indicating the hours[5].

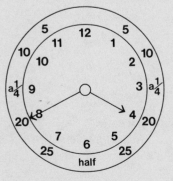

Twenty to four

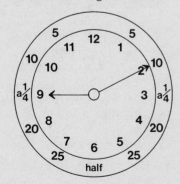

Ten past nine

## 13 Fast and slow

Level **elementary and intermediate**
Age **any**
Group size **whole class, teams, groups**

The class must understand the meaning of *fast* and *slow* in expressions such as *My watch is fast/slow*.

One team is called 'Fast', the other 'Slow', but they should often change titles. The leader of the game calls out a clock time, such as *ten past eight*. If he or she then points to somebody in the 'Fast' team, the response should at once be *a quarter past eight*, if to somebody in the 'Slow' team, *five past eight*, provided the assumption is that five minutes is to be the difference, which will not always be the case.

### Variants

*A* This game can of course be played with simple numbers. If the instruction is, for example, *Add or subtract ten* the 'Fast' team (which could be called the 'Add' team) adds 10 to whatever is called, whereas the 'take away' team subtracts 10. Thus if *20* is called, one team would call *30*, the other *10*.

*B* The game can also be played with weights and measures, distances, temperatures, etc.

## 14 Arrivals[6]

Level **elementary and intermediate**
Age **children**
Group size **whole class, groups**
Use **to practise numbers and clock times, and expressions such as 'by train', 'on foot', etc.**

This is a kind of *Lotto*. Everybody has a card or sheet with, say, six or eight blank clock-faces on it; if necessary the pupils could draw these themselves. The leader of the game says something like *I'm going to London by plane*, to which the class responds with *What time will the plane get there?* The leader then names a time, e.g. *At a quarter to five*, and everybody draws this time in on the first clock-face.

There may be preliminary teaching or revision of expressions such as *by plane/train/car/bicycle/hovercraft/helicopter/ship*, etc. and to help a slow class (and for initial stimulus) there might be a substitution table on the board, e.g.

| I'm going to | the Post Office<br>Edinburgh<br>Sydney<br>Dover<br>the station<br>the moon | by | space-ship<br>bike<br>car<br>plane<br>train<br>boat |
| | | on | foot |

The players need not be restricted by this but encouraged to get away from it.

## 15 Living calendar

Level **elementary**
Age **young children**
Group size **whole class**
Use **to practise dates**

A 'calendar' is marked out on the ground in chalk and each square is numbered, as shown below.

Each child stands in a square. Those in the first line (1–29) are all Sundays, those in the second line, Mondays, and so on. A month is chosen, e.g. July, and anyone can say what date he or she represents: *I am Monday, the ninth of July*, etc.

| 1 | 8 | 15 | 22 | 29 |
| 2 | 9 | 16 | 23 | 30 |
| 3 | 10 | 17 | 24 | 31 |
| 4 | 11 | 18 | 25 | |
| 5 | 12 | 19 | 26 | |
| 6 | 13 | 20 | 27 | |
| 7 | 14 | 21 | 28 | |

Those who are on the 'calendar' can ask each other questions. *Brian, what date is it?* Brian answers with the date he stands for, e.g. *It's Friday, July the twentieth*[7] and asks someone else the same question.

The name of the month should be changed from time to time, and the children can also change places. *Mondays, change with Thursdays* (this means, for July, that one Monday drops out); *first week change with second week*, etc.

If there are more learners than the numbers of days, some can help the teacher with the questioning and some can fill in the odd days of the calendar (e.g. in the above one, the first four days of August).

Here is a rhyme about the days of the week:

> *Solomon Grundy,*      *Worse on Friday,*
> *Born on a Monday,*     *Died on Saturday,*
> *Christened on Tuesday,*   *Buried on Sunday,*
> *Married on Wednesday,*  *That was the end*
> *Ill on Thursday,*          *of Solomon Grundy.*

# 16 Weeks and months

Level **elementary**
Age **children**
Group size **groups, teams, small class**
Use **to practise the names of the days and months**

There are 7, 14, or 21 players in a ring, each named after a day of the week; each day is thus represented exactly once, twice, or three times. (For months of the year the numbers are of course 12 or 24.)

Somebody in the centre throws up a ball and calls out a day (or month) e.g. *Tuesday*. All the 'Tuesdays' run forward and try to catch the ball, after first allowing it to bounce once. The first to catch it, if anyone does, changes with the centre player.

If you think there is a danger of a violent collision, divide the class into rings of 7 (or 12) players only.

## Variant

*Sunday* (or *January*) throws the ball against a wall and names another day (or month) who has to catch it and throw it again, calling on a third player.

# 17 What day of the week?

Level **elementary**
Age **young children**
Group size **small class**
Use **to practise the names of the days of the week**

There are seven large circles, one for each day of the week, preferably marked in large letters on the ground. Everybody (this is suitable only for a small class) stands in one of the circles and says together *What day of the week is it, please?* The leader of the game replies *Friday* (or some other day), at which everybody runs to the Friday circle. As they do so, the leader throws a light ball; anybody it touches before the right circle is reached has to take the leader's place.

If the day where the children are already standing is called, they stay where they are; anyone leaving the circle by mistake has to replace the leader.

# 18 What's the time, Mr Wolf?

Level **elementary**
Age **young children**
Group size **small class, teams, groups**
Use **to practise clock times**

Mr Wolf is confined to a chalk circle on the ground. The others approach one by one and call out *What's the time Mr Wolf?* They are quite safe if he answers *half past three or a quarter to seven,* but whenever he shouts *It's twelve o'clock and my dinner-time* they are in danger and must run away to safety (the walls of the room, the edge of the playground, a certain chalk line, etc.). Anyone touched by Mr Wolf before getting there has to take his place and be a similar menace.

This game should only be played with children who have already learnt to tell the time in their native language.

## Variant

At one end of the playground are the 'sheep' (all the children but

98

two), at the other end the 'shepherd', and in between the 'wolf', who is supposed to be in hiding.

The shepherd calls out *Sheep, sheep, come home.* The sheep answer in despair *No, no, we can't. Why can't you?* asks the shepherd impatiently. *We're afraid. Who are you afraid of? The great big wolf. There isn't any wolf* says the shepherd with scorn. *Sheep, sheep, come home.* Dutifully the sheep make a dash for it and out jumps the wolf. Those who are caught become wolves. The shepherd goes to the other end and the dialogue is repeated.

## Notes and references

1 Odd numbers: 1,3,5,7, etc. Even numbers: 2,4,6,8, etc.
2 Usually pronounced 'two point five', 'three point seven', 'point nought nought one' or 'point oh oh one'.
3 Pronounced 'one pound two ounces/aʊnsɪz/', 'two and a half kilograms'.
4 Pronounced 'three thirty' or 'half past three', 'nine forty-one' or 'nineteen minutes to ten', 'ten fifty-nine' or 'one minute to eleven', and 'two ten' or 'ten (minutes) past two', unless the twenty-four hour clock is used – 15.30 (fifteen thirty), 21.41 (twenty-one forty-one), etc.
5 For constructional details see *Simple Audio-Visual Aids to Foreign-Language Teaching* by W. R. Lee and H. Coppen.
6 Adapted from *Faites Vos Jeux* by M. Buckby and D. Grant, p. 73.
7 This is preferable to *What date are you? I am* . . . which is no use outside the game.

# Chapter 6
# LISTEN-AND-DO GAMES

*The learners have to listen and understand, then carry out some action. Several such games (especially where the main centre of interest is pronunciation, numbers, or spelling) are described in other chapters (see especially Chapters 3–5).*

## 1 Doing what you're told

| | |
|---|---|
| Level | **elementary and intermediate** |
| Age | **children** |
| Group size | **whole class, teams** |
| Use | **to recognise oral commands** |

A command, or a series of commands, is given, which someone, or the whole class, team, or group obeys. e.g. *Touch a window/Jim's coat. Hold up a green book. Point to a tall girl.*

This kind of activity can easily be made into a simple competitive game. The commands are given to different teams in turn, naming those to respond or seeking a collective response. As soon as the action is performed, the other team says either *right* or *wrong*. Team points can be awarded for both commands and responses.

What vocabulary and syntax are used depends on the interests, age-level, and achievement of the class.

### Variants

*A*  Two or more commands may be linked, as in *Go to the door and open it. Clean the board and put the duster on my table. Put these books in the cupboard and then lock it. Change places with Fred and then draw something on the board.*

Ludicrous sequences need not be avoided – it depends on the class. Children often enjoy such things as *Stand on that chair, sing a song, and wink three times*; this may well be an amusing piece of communication which helps to bring the language alive for them, and they will vie with one another in trying to give similar inconsequential commands.

Prepositional phrases slip in readily here, as in *Walk round the room. Jump over my hand. Put this book under Shirley's desk*, etc.

B   Positive and negative commands can be intermingled amusingly, e.g. *Stand up! Sit down! Stand up! Turn to the right! Sit down! Don't stand up! Turn to the left! Hold up your right hand! Turn to the front! Put down your hand!* If there are two teams, they can rapidly be given commands in alternation – and the resulting confusion and laughter will do no harm to motivation. Those who make a mistake have to drop out, but as the game will last only a very short time, and watching the others' antics is itself a pleasure, they will not feel left out in the cold. The team with most members still taking part after x minutes is declared the winner.

C   About six learners face the class, who in turn give commands to them as *quickly* as possible (each should have at least one command ready). All six obey at the same time. If one makes a mistake, he or she drops out and is replaced by somebody from the class.

The teacher is the judge of what commands are reasonable and in reasonable English, but if some of them raise a laugh so much the better.

Examples: *Touch your nose. Turn round three times. Shake hands with the one next to you. Draw a circle on the board. Fold your arms. Put them straight down at your sides. Smile a little. Smile a lot. Brush your hair* (in mime). *Thread a needle* (in mime), etc.

## 2   O'Grady says

| | |
|---|---|
| Level | **elementary and intermediate** |
| Age | **any** |
| Group size | **whole class** |
| Use | **to understand oral commands** |

There is a leader in front of the class (the teacher to begin with) who gives commands, some preceded by the words *O'Grady says* and others not. The class obeys the former only. Thus if the leader says *Touch your noses*, nobody does anything, but if the leader says *O'Grady says touch your noses*, everybody does so at once. Those who make mistakes drop out. The last one left is the winner.

Out of doors there can of course be a broader variety of actions (*Run forward. Take three steps to the left. Jump up and down.*) than if the class is seated at desks, but even in the latter situation there is considerable scope, e.g. *Raise your left hand. Cover your face. Wink twice. Open your mouth. Touch your ears.*

The leader, who should prepare the sequence of commands beforehand, so that the game goes briskly, can perform the actions as he or she gives the orders, even when omitting *O'Grady.*

This is a well-established game which affords a great deal of amusement. It is sometimes played as *Simon Says.*

# 3 Face to face

| | |
|---|---|
| Level | **elementary** |
| Age | **children** |
| Group size | **small class, or groups of about 10 or 12** |
| Use | **to understand simple spoken commands** |

Everybody has a partner, and the two stand facing each other at the circumference of a large circle. Somebody in the centre gives commands which the rest obey, e.g. *Stand back to back. Run round each other. Shake hands three times. Touch each other's shoulders. Turn right round. Touch your toes.* Suddenly the one in the centre shouts *All change* and everybody must quickly get a new partner. The centre player tries to do so too. The one left without a partner goes into the centre and gives commands.

When there is an even number of players, there can be two in the centre.

# 4 Word bingo

| | |
|---|---|
| Level | **elementary and intermediate** |
| Age | **any (except young children)** |
| Group size | **whole class, teams, groups** |
| Use | **to recognize words, letters, or clock times presented orally** |

Everybody has a sheet of paper on which squares have been ruled out, let us say 16 (4 by 4). On the board there is a list of words – altogether 25 or 30 – from which each member of the class chooses 16 to fill in the squares on his or her sheet. (If the class is weak at copying, this stage of the game can take place earlier, giving the teacher time to check.)

The leader of the game calls out words from the list at random and those who have the word on their card cross it out. The first player to have four words in a line or column crossed out calls *Bingo*. A check is necessary.

Vocabulary can be restricted to a single topic, e.g. countries, sports, animals, fruit and vegetables, transport, furniture – whatever goes with the learners' knowledge and interests.

### Variants

*A* The game can be played with letters instead of words. The leader calls out letter-names and the players mark off the letters if they have them on their cards.

*B* It can also be played with clock times. Every card has a number of clock-faces on it, with various times marked on them. Players cover each clock-face with a square of cardboard when they hear the leader say the time it shows.

## 5 True and false

Level **elementary, intermediate, and advanced**
Age **children (Variant C: adults)**
Group size **whole class, teams**
Use **to understand oral statements**

See Chapter 8.11, p. 143. This is a game which can take a number of forms.

There are two chairs (labelled *True* and *False*) in front of the class, and a member of each team is ready to sit on either one or the other. Alternatively, the members of each team are numbered, and the leader of the game calls any number.

Oral statements are made which are obviously true or false, e.g. *It's raining hard* (when the sun is shining). *Richard is absent this morning* (when everybody can see he is present). *There are thirty pupils in this class* (when that is so). *Sylvia is fifteen today. President Carter lives in Canada. Edinburgh is in Scotland,* etc.

If the first representatives of each team (or those who are called by number) think the statement true they hurry to the *True* chair and try to sit on it; if they think it false they make for the *False* chair. The first to sit down fairly and squarely on the right chair gets a team point. Others follow from each team as the next statement is made.

It is important to prepare a list of varied and interesting statements, suited to the ages, interests, and linguistic achievement of the class.

The statements should not be repeated. They can be short and easy, or long and difficult.

The game is most suitable for a fairly small class of, say, 25 pupils or less.

## Variants

*A* The statements can be based on something the class has read, whether fiction or non-fiction. The game then becomes a light-hearted test.

*B* The statements can be limited in some other way also, e.g. to statements about what can be seen in the room, or about the school, or the town, or about what happened the day before or what is going to happen the following week.

Examples of statements about the work of school: *We study French and Spanish as well as English. Our football/basket-ball team has lost only one match this season. The headmaster has been here for seven years. The science laboratory is going to be rebuilt next month,* etc.

Whatever the topic or field of reference, the statements made should not be too easy for the class to take in; otherwise their ability to comprehend is not stretched.

*C* The learners do not move from their places. Instead, they collectively repeat true statements and remain silent for false statements. Or they can simply say *right* or *wrong*. If the teams reply alternately there can be a contest, which makes the matter more interesting.

Statements can also be made about what can be seen in a good clear wall picture: *There are some cows in the field* (*Wrong*). *The footpath leads across the field to the beach* (*Right*), etc. There can be follow up with correct statements: *No, there aren't any cows, but there are some sheep.*

## 6  Told and re-told

| | |
|---|---|
| Level | **advanced** |
| Age | **any (except young children)** |
| Group size | **whole class, groups, pairs** |
| Time taken | **15–40 minutes** |
| Use | **to encourage accurate listening and communication by means of story-telling** |

Four people go out of the room, while the class gets an anecdote or short story ready. This should be an unfamiliar one, but it is preferable if the teacher has one ready to suggest to the class, or those outside may be getting bored.

Back comes No. 1 and is told the story. If it is fairly short, one or two members of the class can tell it, and if it is longer, perhaps four or five, but it should not be very long.

No. 1 listens very carefully, then brings in No. 2 and retells the story as accurately as he can. The class listens and points out any omissions or inaccuracies. No. 2 now brings in No. 3 and tells the story again, with help from No. 1 – this time it goes more quickly and there should be less for the class to correct. Next, No. 3 brings in No. 4 and, helped by Nos. 1 and 2, No. 3 tells the story yet again. Then No. 4 tells it to the class, asking them questions perhaps to make sure of some of the points.

Lastly, members of the class can put questions to all four in order to bring out the full detail, and the story may be retold by others.

Writing may follow.

### Variants

*A*  Two, not four, members of the class go outside. No. 1 returns and is told the story, then goes outside and tells it to No. 2, who returns and tells it to the class. This is a shorter but less interesting procedure.

*B*  One from each group goes outside, while each of the groups gets a story ready. Those outside come back, go to their own groups, and are told the story. Then they visit the other groups and tell it to them.

C   Everybody comes to class ready to tell an anecdote or short story; this could be a joke, something about a personal experience, something read, etc. Ideally every one should be different. The class splits up into pairs so that everybody can tell the story to his colleague. This done, groups of four are formed, but in such a way that nobody is with his pair-mate. (This is easily done if those on the outside of the class change places.) Everybody now retells to the group the story he or she has just heard. A reasonable time is allowed for this and then the class comes together as a whole again, and the teacher asks such questions as *Who has (or has heard) a very funny story? Tell it to us, please. Who has a story about a personal experience?* etc.

This is an excellent 'ice-breaker' for a class which has a fairly good command of the foreign language and the members of which do not know one another. Moreover, the stories told can be made use of on other occasions.

Most of the time during this game should be given to the 'pairs' and 'groups' stages, which usually go with a swing. At the final 'whole class' stage, shyness can show itself, and this stage should be kept fairly short. Language learners are often more willing (if the subject matter is suitable) to talk to one another than to the teacher or to the class as a whole.

# 7   Interruptions

|  |  |
|---|---|
| Level | **advanced (Variant: intermediate and advanced)** |
| Age | **any** |
| Group size | **whole class, groups (Variant: whole class)** |
| Use | **to give practice in asking questions about a story** |

Each group has a story ready. It should not be a familiar one and may be a 'real life' story, e.g. an account of a visit somewhere or of some exceptional happening, or a story of something quite imaginary.

The group faces the class and the leader begins, but members of the class interrupt with questions on points of detail (e.g.

*What time did you start? What was the weather like? What were you wearing? What colour was the bus?*) These questions are answered by other members of the story-teller's group; a certain amount of impromptu invention may be required. Interruptions may be politely made by means of *Excuse me* or *Just a moment, please*. It is unnecessary, and would be unnatural, to use these phrases before every interruption.

### Variant

The teacher tells the story, which is a fairly long one, lasting at least five minutes, but as he goes along he relies upon some of the class to supply detail, asking them questions to obtain this. Thus if the story is about two people who go out for a long walk early one morning, the class may be asked to say what their names are, where they live, what they take with them, what sort of house they live in, what they are wearing, what they see on the way, etc. The class can also ask questions. Here is an exercise in imagination as well as in the use of the foreign language. The details suggested can help to build up an interesting story, which from time to time will need to be recapitulated.

Adaptation to the ages and interests of the learners is of course essential.

## 8 Finding the answers[1]

| | |
|---|---|
| Level | **intermediate** |
| Age | **children** |
| Group size | **whole class, groups** |
| Use | **to help listening and reading comprehension, to practise the use of 'wh'-questions** |

Everybody has a numbered card bearing a question and another numbered card bearing an answer (but not to that question). Altogether there are as many question cards and answer cards as there are members of the class, team, or group. Question cards and answer cards should be of different colours and those which belong together should have the same number. Furthermore, there should be only one answer to each question.

One at a time the members of the class, alternately from the two teams, ask the questions they have on their cards (without mentioning the card number) and name somebody in the other team to reply. If the one named has the right answer he must read it out and give the answer card to the questioner, who checks that the number on the card is the same. If he does not have the right answer card, however, he replies: *Sorry, I don't know*, and it is his turn to ask.

Soon most of the questions and answers will be matched and the team with most pairs of matched cards is the winner.

If the class is a large one, the game is best played in groups. Questions and answers may be based on the general knowledge and interests of the class, on something read, etc. On the whole (in English) they will be questions beginning with *what, where, when, why*, etc.

# 9 Listen and find[2]

| | |
|---|---|
| Level | **elementary** |
| Age | **children** |
| Group size | **whole class** |
| Use | **practice in listening and in naming objects** |

There is a large box or bag and in it a varied assortment of objects of which the class knows the names. The leader of the game looks inside and calls out *There's/I can see a . . . (or some . . . s) in this bag/box. Who can find it/them?*

As the names of the objects are called, children come out in turn from different teams and look for the objects named, which should not be too hard to find. As soon as the object is found, the finder holds it up, says *Here it is/Here they are. I've found it/them. This is a . . ./These are . . . s*, if possible adding a few words of description of size or colour, e.g. *It's an apple, it's a small green apple . . . It's a button, it's a big black button.*

A team point can be awarded to every correct identification. Those who cannot find the object and hold up the wrong one must give way to a member of the opposite team.

## 10 Listen and draw

Level **elementary and intermediate**
Age **any**
Group size **whole class, pairs, groups**
Use **to understand instructions**

Everybody has a sheet of paper and draws what the leader of the game tells them to do. For example: *Draw a triangle on the left-hand side near the top . . . Now draw a circle of about the same size just below it . . . Draw a long line across the paper, near the bottom . . . Put a bigger circle on the right-hand side of the paper . . . Now draw an upright line between the triangle and the big circle . . . Print your name inside the bigger circle.*

The class, if shown the key, can correct their own paper.

The instructions can of course be made a little easier or a lot more difficult. Buildings, vehicles, and people (matchstick figures) can be drawn.

### Variants

*A* The same kind of activity can be carried on in pairs. The two are divided by a screen of some sort, e.g. a pile of books, so that they cannot see each other's papers. A tells B what to do, step by step, and vice versa. The resulting drawings can be discussed, e.g. A: *This circle is in the wrong place.* B: *Where did you tell me to put it?* A: *On the left, not on the right*, etc.

*B* As for A, but in groups of four, two on one side of the 'screen' and two on the other. Partners alternate in giving instructions.

# 11 Hullo, who are you?

| | |
|---|---|
| Level | **elementary** |
| Age | **children** |
| Group size | **whole class** |
| Use | **to practise greetings and responses** |

One member of each team (say, Nigel and Caroline) goes to the front and faces the board. Pupils in the class, either in some prearranged order in alternation between teams, or as pointed to by the leader of the game, say *Hullo, Nigel and Caroline*, or alternatively, *Good morning/afternoon*. Nigel and Caroline have to say who has spoken (e.g. *That's Chris*) and the first to do so wins a team point.

More may be said, e.g. *How do you do, Nigel and Caroline?* or *Hullo, Nigel and Caroline, how ARE you?* Possible replies: *How do you do, Chris? Very well, Chris, how are YOU?*

# 12 Noticing nonsense

| | |
|---|---|
| Level | **intermediate** |
| Age | **mainly children** |
| Group size | **whole class** |
| Use | **to encourage careful listening** |

The teacher, or one of the learners in turn, makes nonsensical statements to the class. They are easy to correct, however, since there is only one silly word. The learners are asked haphazard, but alternating between teams, to put the sentences right.

Examples: *The sun rises in the west. An orange is square. We go to bed in the morning. On very cold days we put on our swimsuits. Cows live in flats. Ice-cream is hot. People play the guitar with their noses.* Bright pupils can invent more such statements and try them out in the game.

## Variants

The teacher reads a short story or description which contains statements similar to those above. Pupils raise their hands when they hear nonsense, and must be able to correct it.

**Example:** *We were all on a ship, and there was a very bad storm. The ship struck a lamp-post and broke in two. But then we saw a garage. The sailors got into the boats and cycled away. My wife and I and our four grandmothers were alone on the ship with a hundred people. The children's names were Jack, Ernest, Mary, and Kate; one was a boy and the others were girls, and they were all 60 years old. In the morning there was no wind at all and the sea was rough. There was a fog. The sun was shining brightly, so we put on our pyjamas and went to bed. We built a boat out of bottle-tops. Then we got into our tent and walked across the water to the island. We found a wet place and lit a fire with banana skins. Nearby we heard some monkeys calling 'Cock-a-doodle-doo'. The next day it was hot, so we ran about in the tree-tops to get warm.*

## Notes and references

1 Adapted from *Guide de l'Assistant de Français* by G. Fontier and M. le Cunff.
2 Adapted from *Language Teaching Analysis* by W. F. Mackey.

# Chapter 7
# READ-AND-DO-GAMES

*Foreign language and second language learners may need pre-reading activities, some of them in order to discover what reading is and others to relearn the direction of reading. One kind of pre-reading material is a picture story which can only be understood if it is followed across from left to right and down the page. Another kind is quite simply an attractive book with interesting pictures, which will make children (and adults too, if they cannot yet read)* want *to read.*

*We are concerned in this book mainly with those who can read at least to some extent in their native language, who can speak a little in the foreign or second language, and who have had at least some training in left-to-right reading if they needed it.*

*True reading is not a matter of laborious letter-by-letter or syllable-by-syllable decipherment, as if one were faced with a manuscript written in an unknown language. Nor should reading be identified with reading aloud. A reader has read a sentence or passage well who has fully grasped its meaning, whether the text is then spoken or not.*

*This does not, of course, mean that there is no place for reading aloud in a foreign language course. In the earliest stages of reading, the teacher's oral aid is necessary if meaning is to be found in print. Then and later, also, there is some printed material which demands to be read (or rather, spoken) aloud.*

*Both sentence-recognition and word-recognition skills need to be developed, and the latter include the ability to read parts of words and to discriminate between letters. Recognition of the 'linking' words and phrases which make a succession of sentences cohere in a meaningful whole is also essential. Only when all these skills have been acquired can a reader read without help, at least within the bounds of his or her knowledge and experience. Given interesting texts which are not too difficult, such a reader can go ahead alone. It is a wonderful moment for language learners when they realize they can do this. Not all of them, alas, get so far.*

*Reading games belong mainly to the early stages of reading, although treasure hunts and the like (see page 124) may demand a more advanced achievement.*

*In the earliest stages of reading, flashcards, if used properly, are a great help, especially to children. Flashcards are simply cards which are 'flashed' at the class, i.e. shown to the class briefly. On them are printed sentences or words, large enough to be seen clearly from the back of the class.*

*Here then, are a few ways of using flashcards. Sentence-cards come first, sentences being the main vehicle of communication.*

# 1 Games with flashcards (Sentences)

Level **elementary**
Age **children**
Group size **whole class, groups**
Use **to respond quickly to a familiar command or question presented in the unfamiliar medium of print**

1.1 *Commands.* The learners are accustomed to giving and obeying these commands orally, and now they meet them in print and learn to recognize them as wholes. The cards bear such commands as: *Open the door. Shut the window. Stand up. Turn round. Go to the door. Leave the room. Walk round the room. Sing a song. Brush your hair. Draw a house,* etc. The more sentences like this you have on cards the better. They should be varied, there should be repetition of words, and some of them should be amusing.

The leader of the game holds up a card for a moment or two, waits until several pupils have put their hands up, and names someone, who performs the action required. If the card is mis-read and the wrong or no action performed, there will be others eager to show they have understood it, and somebody in another team is given a chance.

As soon as someone has responded correctly to the card, the teacher (or a pupil leading the game) can ask *What does the card say?* and the class can repeat what is on it. But the normal response to a command is to carry it out, not to repeat it, and this is what should first be done.

The cards should be held above the eye-level of the class and should be presented briskly, so that the game does not drag.

It is an advantage to have the sentences pencilled in small letters on the back of the cards, so that those holding them up do not have to turn them round to remind themselves of what they are showing. The order of showing should, of course, be decided on in advance and cards suitably arranged, otherwise there will be uncertain fumbling with the pile of cards.

This type of game can also be played in groups, arranged in semicircles. One player, standing in the centre, shows commands in turn to others.

1.2   *Questions.* Questions also call for a response, whether they are spoken or printed. The cards bear questions such as: *What's this?* (one end of the card may be given an arrowhead shape, to point at objects near which it is held), *Where's my hat?* (*It's on your table/head*, etc.). *What's the time?* (for use with a real or cardboard clock). *Who's this?* (*It's George/Barbara*, etc.). For this activity *wh*-questions are preferable to *yes-no* questions.

### Variants

*A*   Team A has question cards (at least one each) and Team B the corresponding answer cards. In some prearranged order, or as named, As hold up a question and Bs the appropriate answer, both doing so from the front of the class.

*B*   Question-cards may be shown by those in one team and answers orally by those in another.

Command-cards may be used in a similar way.

## 2   Games with flashcards (Words)

| | |
|---|---|
| Level | **elementary** |
| Age | **children** |
| Group size | **whole class, groups** |
| Use | **to respond quickly to a familiar command or question presented in the unfamiliar medium of print** |

114

First reading in the foreign language is meaningful to the learners if it is based on communicative exchanges, e.g. command and response, question and answer, as under 1 above. But *word recognition* has also got to be developed. As soon as the learners can read without much difficulty the sentences used in the earliest flashcard games, methodical training in word recognition can begin.

Flashcard games with *words* will not be described in detail. They are similar to flashcard games with sentences, although the aim is different. Indeed, sentence-cards should be used, but instead of differing very much from one another (so that recognition of the sentence as a whole is comparatively easy) they differ by only one word, as do *Touch the table* and *Touch the cupboard* or *Touch my coat* and *Touch my desk* (here the two words are the same length and harder to distinguish visually). We can carry the matter further, to the stage of letter recognition, by using sentences which are the same except for a single letter-group or letter, as are *Give me a pen* and *Give me a pin. Draw a bear* and *Draw a bean. Point to the sun* (in a picture) and *Point to the son. Touch your boots* and *Touch your books. Where is your hat?* and *Where is your hut?* Small visual differences such as these (there may be no auditory difference) oblige the learners to look at words and letters closely.

Reading work with words and letters alone is liable to be much less interesting because meaning is further away.

# 3 Matching games

|            |                                                              |
|------------|--------------------------------------------------------------|
| Level      | **elementary**                                               |
| Age        | **children**                                                 |
| Group size | **whole class, teams, groups, individuals**                  |
| Use        | **to encourage accurate silent reading of sentences (Variant I: to encourage accurate word recognition)** |

Sentences or phrases are matched to pictures or objects and vice versa. The cards are not 'flashed' but are just placed under or against the object or picture. Sentences like *This is a house*, *This is Red Riding Hood*, or *This is a chair* are the simplest. With some pictures longer sentences are possible such as *John and his sister are waving goodbye* or *The little girl has fallen into the water*. A large supply of sentences is necessary.

For this type of activity it is an advantage to have a collection of simple pictures showing the object or action. They can be backed with sandpaper or felt, and attached or removed from a flannel-board in a moment. The sentence-cards can be similarly backed. If the picture is more complicated, the detail must be visible to the whole class and there should be room underneath it for a number of sentence-cards describing what can be seen: a large flannelboard is therefore necessary.

The picture is shown and a descriptive sentence obtained from the class, e.g. *Barbara is skipping*. The card bearing this sentence is then put underneath. Similarly for other pictures. Then the game can begin. The sentence-cards are given out. The teacher puts up the first picture once more and asks a question, e.g. *What is Barbara doing? She's skipping*, everybody says, and the pupil with the right card comes out and puts it with the picture. The other pictures are dealt with in the same way, and all are left up. A team point can be given to everyone who produces the right sentence-card promptly. At the end there can be group or class reading of all the sentences; do not let them be chanted in a monotonous sing-song – young children are apt to do this.

## Variants

*A* The pictures, not the sentences, are given out, and the sentences put up. As the sentences are shown, they are read silently and the right picture is brought forward and put with them. After a time, the class can be told *Now let's see whether we can do this without saying a single word. No point for the team if I hear anybody whispering*.

*B* Questions such as *What's this? What's he doing?* or *What is he going to do?* can be put up on the board or flannelboard with certain pictures. Answer-cards have been given out and the pupils supply the right one for each picture.

*C* The pictures can be given out to one team and the state-ment cards to another. The pupils in turn, and alternately from the two teams, come to the front and hold up (either as they are named or in some prearranged order) a picture or a statement-card, so that everybody can see it. If it is a statement, somebody in the other team then brings out and shows the picture that goes with it, and if it is a picture, the matching sentence. Together the two put up sentence and picture on the board.

D Matching can also be done as an individual activity. Everybody has some sentences and pictures, matches them as quickly as possible, and then exchanges them for another set. A point can be given for each set completed.

If each set of pictures tells a simple story, interest is stimulated. A series of six sentences to go with six pictures might, for instance, be: *Paul is getting up. He is washing himself. Now he is dressing. He is eating his breakfast. He is leaving his house. He is running to school.*

E An interesting game can be played if some of the sentences a learner has can only be matched with pictures in another one's possession. First, the learners match what they can, and the teacher should have arranged things so that everybody has about the same number that can be matched. Then the teams exchange one card they have been unable to match, each player exchanging with the nearest member of another team. *Here's one of my cards. Please give me one of yours.* Either pictures or sentences are exchanged, not both. Matching continues. There is another exchange, but not with the same person as before. When all of a player's cards have been matched, he or she says *I'm ready* or raises a hand. The game continues until most in one team have matched all their cards.

F There are several sets of sentence-cards and of the picture-cards that go with them. The teacher has one set. Each of the other sets is given to a group, but the cards are mixed up and put in a heap on a desk. The groups sit or stand round their desk. The teacher holds up cards in turn, and a member – a different one each time – of *each* group looks either for the corresponding picture-card or for the corresponding sentence-card. The first to find it scores a point. Some of the sentences and pictures should closely resemble one another.

G There are picture-cards (or sentence-cards) hidden about the room, and everybody has a sentence-card if picture-cards have been hidden, or a picture-card if sentence-cards have been hidden. The game is to find the picture (or the sentence) that goes with what one has. Pupils return to their seats with both cards as soon as they find what they are looking for. The first team with all its members back is the winner. This is a game for a fairly small class (say, twenty) where there is room to move about.

*H* A number of picture-cards and an equal number of cards bearing the corresponding words are needed. One member of the group, after mixing the cards, spreads them out face downwards on a desk or table. The first player turns any two cards face upwards, so that everybody can see them. If the two cards match (e.g. if one of them is a picture of a ship and the other is the phrase *a ship*) this player takes them both and then turns up another two cards. If the two cards do not match in this way, they are turned face downwards again. One after another the players turn up two cards, trying of course to remember the whereabouts of certain cards which have been turned up and then turned down again.

The game continues until all the cards have been matched. The player with most cards is the winner[1].

*I Sentence Line.* There are many large cards with words on them from which sentences interesting to young children can be made, e.g. *Teddy Bear is going to the beach. Cinderella lost her slipper. Yesterday we went for a walk in the fields* – whatever harmonizes with what they have been reading or doing or hearing about. These word-cards are in a pile on a table in front of the class.

The teacher writes a sentence, high up, across the board. Learners from one group each find one word of this sentence in the pile and stand with the card below the corresponding word on the board. If there are not enough learners in the first group to account for all the words in the sentence, the next group helps them. Other groups read the sentence aloud. Next time it will be their turn to line up.

# 4 Rhymes and songs

| | |
|---|---|
| Level | **elementary** |
| Age | **any (especially children)** |
| Group size | **whole class** |
| Use | **to develop visual skills of phrase and word identification** |

These offer a pleasant and effective approach to reading and can be used in addition to sentence-cards etc. (see under **1** to **3** above). This way of getting to grips with the foreign language alphabet is very different.

If the pupils cannot already say or sing the rhyme, it is first taught orally. It should be fairly simple. If some words occur in it several times, that is an advantage, as it can be used for word-recognition as well as phrase and line-recognition, though the first thing is to recognize the lines.

Here is one example, a well-known song popular with both children and adults.

> My bonnie[2] is over the ocean,
> My bonnie is over the sea,
> My bonnie is over the ocean,
> Oh, bring back my bonnie to me.
> Bring back, bring back,
> Bring back my bonnie to me, to me;
> Bring back, bring back,
> Oh bring back my bonnie to me.

(And so on. The other verses can also be used.)[3]

The main thing is that the song should be liked and already more or less known. The teacher says it and sings it with the learners and then they sing it again, looking at the large sheet or board on which it is written. The teacher points to the lines as the song is sung right through without stopping. First it is the teacher who points and then one or two of the learners.

The next step is *line* identification. *Point to 'Oh, bring back my bonnie to me'* says the teacher. *Good. Sing it . . . Point to 'My bonnie is over the ocean . . .' Yes. Who can see 'Bring back, bring back?' Right. Here, and again here.* And so on. This is simple enough when the lines are arranged in the order in which they have to be sung.

But now, on another wall-sheet or board, we have lines in a different order, mixed up something like this:

> Bring back, bring back,
> My bonnie is over the sea,
> Oh, bring back my bonnie to me.
> My bonnie is over the ocean, etc.

Use other verses too. This has been prepared beforehand but has not been visible to the learners.

The song is now sung through again (in the normal line order of course) and the teacher points to the printed lines in the jumbled version as each line is sung. Then one or two members of the class can do this.

Certainty of line identification may not be reached at once. That does not matter. Nor does it matter at this stage if the learners identify lines by their length or, in some instances, by punctuation, for proficient readers do and must take such features into account whenever they read.

But this is not yet much like fully proficient reading. There are further steps to be taken – and especially the recognition of individual *words*. This is where verses in which words occur several times come in useful. Such words, so much more meaningful in a context than alone, are pointed out, and then pupils locate them too. *Who can find 'ocean'? Yes, that's right. Now who can find another 'ocean'?* This sort of activity is particularly useful to those familiar with an entirely different alphabet for their first language. Speakers of languages which are written in the Latin alphabet should imagine the above procedure as applied to the reading of Chinese, Hebrew, or Arabic.

Not only can the lines be jumbled, but also the words in a line. This is not so helpful, however, for we read to a large extent in phrases and therefore should not destroy the visual pattern of the phrase.

It is best to have a number of these verses or songs, with the lines in the right order, printed out on sheets, so that they can be used on several occasions and be ready the following year. For quick rearrangement of the lines in various orders, a large flannelboard is convenient; if the cardboard on which the separate lines are printed is backed with sandpaper, the lines can be moved about with ease.

## 5 Stepping-stones

Level **elementary**
Age **young children**
Group size **whole class, teams**
Use **reading/pronunciation practice (words)**

See Chapter 3.8, p. 59. Here the words are read (preferably in a phrase or short sentence) and not spelt. If a word is read correctly, it is written on a stone and the reader or the reader's team makes progress across the river.

The words should be those the children have been speaking and writing.

## 6 Living sentences

Level **elementary**
Age **young children**
Group size **whole class, teams**
Use **reading practice (sentences and words)**

See Chapter 3.5. Instead of letter-cards the children have word-cards and go to the front of the class to form sentences given by the leader. If the sentences are short and there is enough space, two or more teams can form the sentence simultaneously.

## 7 Word snap

Level **elementary**
Age **children (Variants: any)**
Group size **groups**
Use **to practise quick word recognition (Variant: to encourage quicker reading and prompt speaking of clock-time phrases)**

Cards the size of playing-cards bear words (on one side only, but both ways up) which pupils have had some difficulty in recognizing. The game is played in groups of 4 to 6. There is a pack of up to 60 cards, bearing about 12 different words, for each group. The cards are given out haphazard and in equal numbers to each player, and each takes it in turn to begin. The players one by one put down a card in front of them, words upwards. They go on doing this, placing the cards on those they have played, until one of the cards is seen to be the same as another one. Anybody can then call *Snap* and the first to do so collects all the cards the two players concerned have already put down. (Alternatively, only these two players themselves can say *Snap*.)

A number of words in the pack should differ in appearance from one another only slightly, e.g. by one letter (*wood/food, pig/big, small/smell, monkey/donkey,* etc.)

If the word-cards are designed like this:

| | |
|---|---|
| **believe** | **laugh** |
| **əʌəᴉləq** | **ɥɓnɐl** |

there should be little difficulty in seeing quickly what is on them.

## Variant

*Snap with clock times.* There are many cards with clock times marked on them as well as the words *What's the time?* (or *What time is it?*). *It's* (whatever the clock-face shows). It is helpful if both the words and the clock-face appear twice on the card, so that it can easily be read from more than one angle of view. The words should be more prominent than the clock-face.

The cards are distributed to all the members of the group. Each in turn puts down a card face upwards on a single pile. Whenever a card put down is the same as the one before, the first player to say aloud the time indicated picks up the cards.

## Variant

Once this game has become familiar it can be played with cards which do not have clock-faces. It is then a pure reading game.

# 8 Word and sentence lotto

Level **elementary**
Age **children**
Group size **whole class, teams, groups**
Use **to encourage quick word recognition**

Each pupil has a word-card on which there are several words arranged under one another (see diagram).

If the learners' vocabulary is extensive enough, everybody can have a more or less different set of words. For a class of 30, this means finding 120–150 words which are not too easy to read. They can be typed on paper and stuck on the cards.

Small single-word strips, one for every word on the cards, are put on a tray or in a bowl or bag. If certain words occur a number of times on the cards, there must be corresponding repetition of these words on the strips.

The leader of the game takes one of the strips at a time and either reads it out or (for a small class) shows it. Anybody who has the same word on his card as

| |
|---|
| **engine** |
| **flight** |
| **early** |
| **descent** |
| **airport** |

he sees on the teacher's strip can claim the strip by putting up his hand and saying the word. If two claim a word, the first to do so gets it. The game goes along briskly, with only a few seconds between each word. The first team to have all its words covered is the winner.

## Variant

Pupils have sentence-cards instead of word-cards. Each is different, but there are some words on several cards. The leader of the game (the teacher, to begin with) has word-strips and reads out or shows the words one by one. Pupils claim any words which appear in their sentences.

# 9 Carrying out orders

Level **elementary, intermediate, and advanced**
Age **children, possibly modifiable for adults**
Group size **whole class, teams, groups**
Use **action-linked practice in reading**

Various commands are written or printed on numbered cards.
Members of the class draw numbers from a hat or box, find the
card which has the same number, and perform the action.

The commands may be simple or complicated, e.g. *Open a
window. Draw an umbrella on the board. Ask somebody what the
time is. If there is anybody wearing a pullover, tell him to sit near the
window.* A whole message or anecdote, which has to be relayed
to an individual or to the class, may indeed be found on the card.
Thus the game can be suited to the class's interests and abilities.

## Variants

*A* As above, except that the commands themselves are on the
board or a wall-sheet, and thus visible to the whole class. The
advantage of this variant is that most pupils are then reading
most of the time, and wondering which of the commands they
will get. But there is less surprise!

*B* Also as above, except that there is no drawing of numbers.
Cards bearing commands are drawn and the commands are
carried out. The class can then be asked *What was on the
card? What did the card say?*

*C* Numbered commands are on a visible list. The leader of
the game calls a number and also a learner's name. The learner
reads the sentence silently and performs the action.[4]

# 10 Treasure hunt

Level **intermediate and advanced**
Age **children and teenagers**
Group size **whole class, and groups**
Use **reading practice (directions)**

In order to find the 'treasure', the players must be able to read the
clues, and these are hidden about the room or in various places

out of doors. (Schools lucky enough to have grounds sometimes organize quite elaborate foreign language treasure hunts.)[5]

The 'treasure' may be a good book or pen, sweets, or some sort of toy, or possibly only team points. It depends very much on the learners' ages, but it should be something they would like to have.

There is a different set of numbered clues, marked a different colour or perhaps in envelopes bearing a group's name or number, for every group. Each group is given an initial clue, and these clues should lead on one to another, for example thus: *Look under the window and find a box*. The group do so and discover the second clue inside: *Go to the cupboard and take out an atlas*. They find a message in the atlas: *Follow the chalk line which leads to the back of the room*. What chalk line? Ah, here it is – a faint one on the floor. They follow it, and at the back of the room there is a small coin on a ledge. Under it, on a small scrap of paper, is the next clue: *Face east and find the arrow*. They face west and find nothing. Presently they realize the mistake and see the arrow marked on the side of a picture on the wall. It points downwards. In the basket underneath there is the last clue: *You will find the treasure two metres from here*. It turns out to be in a box on the table.

Indoors, unless the classroom is spacious, this is an activity for a small class. It should be played by small groups (say, of three or four), each group following a different set of clues. But all the clues must lead, by different routes, to the same 'treasure'. The clues should be silently written down by everybody as they are found.

Outdoors the clues may be more numerous. What they are depends on the nature of the surroundings.

Careful preparation is required, and once the general idea is grasped, everybody will enjoy taking an active part. Indeed, a group of clue-makers and clue-placers can be formed, which will not itself take part in the treasure hunt.

Play the game once or twice a year, and keep the best clues for the next year.

## Variants

*A* An easier, though perhaps less interesting, way of organizing a treasure hunt is to hide various small objects, of which the learners have a list, about the room or playground.

Small groups find these and make a note of the word attached to each one. Together these words make a sentence saying where the treasure is. The first group to find it is the winner.

B Some of the clues can be in the form of sentences with mixed word order (*Look of third cupboard shelf the on the*), riddles (*I have hands and a face but no head. Look near me.* i.e. near the clock).

# 11 Tasks

Level **elementary and intermediate**
Age **children**
Group size **whole class, teams**
Use **reading practice (commands and questions)**

A number of 'letters' (folded pieces of paper) are hidden beforehand about the room, though they should be fairly easy to find. They are marked with a different colour for each team, and there must be enough for every pupil to have one. Each 'letter' contains a task which calls for successful reading, e.g. answering a question, completing a sentence, performing an action. Everyone has to find a 'letter' marked with the right team colour and carry out the task.

In a small class there could be two or more tasks for everybody. The game can be suited to classes at various standards of reading achievement, by making the task less or more complicated.

Examples of tasks demanding performance: *Dust the table. Clean the board. Change the water in the vase. Open the window wider. Take a book out of the cupboard. Throw away the dead flowers.* As a lot of things will be going on at the same time, avoid comical tasks unless you want a lot of noise and confusion.

Questions: *How old are you? When is your birthday? What is the weather like today? How many pictures are there in this room? How many brothers and sisters has X got? (Ask her/him).* Brief answers are written.

As soon as the class is seated the teacher can briefly ask for some 'letters' to be read out, and ask, for instance, *Did you dust it? Where is the chalk now?* or *What did you write? And what is the weather like?* etc.

## 12 Did you find it?

Level **intermediate and advanced**
Age **children**
Group size **whole class**
Use **reading (and possibly) writing practice: revision of certain prepositions of place and of vocabulary**

Everybody has a list of objects to be found and a bag in which to put them. The objects might include a box of used matches, two small green buttons, a clean handkerchief, a paper-clip, an unused stamp, a wrapped sweet, a pair of shoelaces, and so on – the more objects the better.

The collectors search here, there, and everywhere – in and behind cupboards, in drawers, behind and under books and bags, etc. It is best if they search in pairs, so that one can make a quick note of where the objects are found. The time allowed should be limited. The winning pair is the one with the most objects in their bag.

### Variants

*A* Instead of a list of objects only, they can have a list of sentences describing objects and giving hints as to where they might be found; e.g. *There are two small green buttons in different places – one is under something and the other inside something.*

*B* After finding as many objects as possible in five minutes, the searcher(s) sit down and write where they have found them; e.g. *Well found the packet of tea on the second shelf of the cupboard, behind a pile of history books.* A further ten minutes is allowed for this.

*C* Groups can prepare lists for each other.

*D* The sentences state where the objects are to be found but not what they are; e.g. *Inside one of the green books there is a —*
*——.* The searchers have to find the objects and complete the sentences.

*E* Other things apart from such objects may have to be found. *Find out on what day of the week Christmas Day falls next year. Find something hard and square. Find something that smells sweet. Find something the name of which begins with B,* etc.

# 13 Reconstructing the story

Level **intermediate and advanced**
Age **any (except young children)**
Group size **groups**
Use **practice in reading sentences in the light of their relationship in meaning to other sentences**

An anecdote or short story (at least, say, ten sentences long) is cut up into sentences (and even phrases), and each sentence is pasted on a strip of card. Two or more of these strips are given to each member of the group. Under the group leader's guidance the learners read out their sentences and then try to put them into the right order. *Which sentence comes first? Mine* says Dick. *Read it out. Who thinks that sentence comes first? Everybody? Nobody? Read yours, Sarah. Who thinks Sarah's sentence comes first? All right, give it to me.* The leader reads out the first sentence. Then the second is found and the two are read. And so on, until the story is reconstructed.

## Variants

*A* Groups can themselves cut up stories and give them to other groups to put together.

*B* At a relatively elementary level the teacher can give the learners an idea in advance of the general lines of the story.

*C* At a relatively advanced level one group can have *some* of the sentences of the story and another group the rest. So they cannot make a complete story, and have to communicate group to group in order to sort out the problem.

## 14 Fortunes

Level **intermediate**
Age **children**
Group size **groups**
Use **reading practice (especially using 'will')**

The group has a wheel, consisting of a large circle and pointer attached firmly to a piece of wood or strong cardboard. Round the circumference are numbers. Each player spins the pointer. The number at which it is pointing when it comes to rest is looked up in the key kept by one of the players (the fortune-teller). The 'fortune' is read out – *You will make a long journey some time. Next week we shall all have a day's holiday* (schools usually do). *Unless you eat less you will get very fat.*

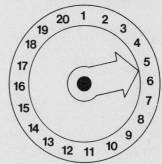

The teacher, preferably with the learners' help, should have prepared these 'fortunes' carefully to suit their ages and interests.

## 15 Answers and questions

There are two sets of cards, one bearing questions and the other the answers to these questions, and each learner has one card only, which may be either a question or an answer.

If you have a question, the game is to find who has the answer to it; if you have an answer, to find who has the question. So the teacher says *Go* or *Begin*, and the 'questions' and 'answers' seek one another out. This means moving about the room and (in English) asking such questions as *Have you (got) a question/answer? What is it? Can I see it, please?* and commenting *No, that's no good. Good – that's the answer to my question – that's the question for my answer*, etc.

Finally, the 'questions' stand with their 'answers', show their cards, and read them aloud.

Depending on the level and interests of the learners, the questions and answers can be based on general knowledge, on a story all have read, or on some limited field of vocabulary (e.g. countries and languages, colours and sizes, shopping, etc.)

## Variant

Group leaders have the questions, members of the group the answers. When the question is read out, the learner who has the right answer-card reads it aloud and hands the card to the group leader.[6]

# 16 Scrambled lines

Level **intermediate and advanced**
Age **any (except young children)**
Group size **whole class**
Use **to practise identifying links between one sentence or phrase and another**

All the lines of several fairly familiar songs are put on slips of paper, one line on each slip, and these are distributed to the players, one each. The game is to find those who have the other lines of the song, and then sing it together, before another group sings one of the other songs.

## Variant

The same kind of thing may be done with printed conversations or dialogues. They can be cut up into sections and distributed at random. The game is to find who has the other phrase(s) or sentence(s) that go with one's own. Here are some examples of simple conversational exchanges which could be split up.

A. *I say, you've taken my coat, haven't you?*
B. *Oh, have I? I'm very sorry, it looks just like mine.*

A. *Are you likely to be at the meeting tonight?*
B. *Well, I'm not sure. I might get along.*

A. *Excuse me, smoking isn't allowed here.*
B. *Sorry, but what can I do about it?*
A. *You could put it out.*

B. *I'll get in another carriage at the next station.*
A. *Meanwhile we have to put up with it, I suppose.*

A. *Do you think you could make a bit less noise? I can't hear a thing.*
B. *All right. What time does it finish?*

A. *That will be £2.50.*
B. *Haven't you made a mistake?*
A. *I'll add it up again. No, that's right.*
B. *Will you accept a cheque?*

# 17 Snakes and ladders

| | |
|---|---|
| Level | **elementary, intermediate, and advanced** |
| Age | **any** |
| Group size | **groups** |
| Use | **reading and speaking practice.** |

See Chapter 9.18, Variant p. 167.

## Notes and references

1 This game, in various forms, is described in *Programmed Instruction for Literacy Workers* by Sivasailam Thiagarajan, International Institute for Adult Literacy Methods, pp. 116–17.
2 A Scottish dialect word, meaning here 'sweetheart' or 'true-love'.
3 The full words can be found in *Time for a Song* by W. R. Lee and M. Dodderidge, which contains other songs of this type, e.g. *London Bridge, I Saw Three Ships, The Animals Went in Two by Two*. Well-known pop songs can also be used. Many learners will be anxious to see and read the words.
4 See *Language Teaching Analysis* by W. F. Mackey, pp. 450–1.
5 J. Klyhn in 'Hunting for Treasure in English', *Modern English Teacher* 4, 3, 1976, describes a version for adult learners which enlists the help of people living in the neighbourhood, who must be willing to give out information, respond to passwords, or give out envelopes containing messages.
6 Adapted from *Faites vos Jeux* by M. Buckby and D. Grant, p. 24.

# Chapter 8
# GAMES AND
# WRITING

*Most of the games so far described are oral, with writing in some instances as an optional follow-up or incidental aspect of the game. For young children, moreover, writing is slow and laborious, if they can write at all. Nevertheless in many types of game writing can, for instance, help with the preparation of oral questions (e.g. in Alibi, and in hiding and searching games). Vocabulary games can have a written accompaniment, e.g. noting down items added to the list. 'Reminder' words and phrases may also be committed to paper. Spelling is essentially an aspect of writing and so writing is involved with some of the games in Chapter 3. Writing can readily be added to many of the Read-and-Do games in Chapter 7.*

*Experienced language teachers are familiar in practice with the fact that the traditional language skills — listening, reading, speaking, writing — are interrelated, although this interrelationship has been insufficiently studied. The strengthening of one of those skills, once a certain stage of proficiency in using the language has been reached, tends to strengthen the others. Games which involve several of the skills perhaps have, therefore, a special value. In this book there are many such, although they have been classified according to their main characteristic.*

*The main characteristic of the games which follow is writing. The first reading should, ideally, be the reading of whole sentences and longer stretches of language which the learners can already speak, i.e. which mean something to them. It is convenient, unless the learners are very young and have not begun to write in their first language or find writing very laborious indeed, for writing in the foreign language to begin soon after reading.*

*Writing is a sort of reading too, unless it is wholly mechanical copying — one reads (i.e. looks at and understands) what one writes. But in writing the learners are preoccupied with letters from the start. They have to write them and join them together into written words, and doing this means looking at them closely. Thus it seems preferable on the whole not to introduce writing in the foreign language until early reading instruction has reached a stage at which the learners notice small differences (e.g. one-letter differences) between words (see p. 114). However, it has to be recognized that many language teachers introduce writing from the very first lesson, on the assumption that it is best even at the beginning for all the language skills to be taught: and there is something to be said for this if the lesson periods are very long or if the learners can already write with some ease in their native language.*

*The simplest form of written work is copying. Let it be done in the same letters as print. Cursive handwriting can wait, though this does not apply to learners whose first language uses the same alphabet as the foreign language and who have already mastered a similar difference between print and cursive in the former.*

*Note: In all the games below, the use is to encourage meaningful writing practice.*

# 1 Lively letters

|          |                                  |
|---------:|----------------------------------|
| Level    | **elementary**                   |
| Age      | **young children**               |
| Group size | **whole class, teams, groups** |
| Use      | **to make the letter-shapes familiar** |

The earliest writing games may be friendly competitions in the spirit of 'Let's see who can make letters best.' For young children the letters could be made to look like people or animals or objects. S, for example is like a snake, T is an umbrella or (if lowered) a table[1]. A is like a hut or (upside down) an ox's head, C is a new moon, D (like this ⌓) is a sort of hat, V is a tent upside down, small h is a chair to sit on, d and b are like two sentries outside a gate (N), O can be given features and two letters o are his children, q and p are d and b standing on their heads, or d, b, q, and p live in a little square house (two upstairs and two downstairs).

**dNb**

Moreover, if d rolls over in bed he is b, and if q rolls over he is p. R is P being held up by \ because he is tired, H is a rugby football goal or a jumping stand, j is i with a tail, n is the entrance to a railway tunnel, Z is an N which has fallen over on its side, o can be a hole in something, f is a plant bending over at the top, and so on. Once more, the inventive teacher ... And it amuses the teacher too.

## 2 Stepping-stones

See Chapter 3.8, p. 59. Stepping-stones may be adapted as a writing game.

|  |  |
|---:|:---|
| Level | **elementary** |
| Age | **young children** |
| Group size | **whole class** |

The learners copy certain words from the board on to the stones. All who do so correctly have crossed the river without slipping – those who have slipped more than twice were in danger of being eaten by the crocodiles. And now, having reached the other side, we make our way back to our camp via another set of words. Similarly with *Ladders*, etc. (p. 166).

# 3 Completing the sentences

Level **intermediate and advanced**
Age **any (except young children)**
Group size **groups**

This may be little more than copying, but an element of friendly competition can increase effort and interest.

If the missing words are to be found elsewhere – possibly on a notice-board or the back of a movable board – and the work is being done in groups, the group can look at each sentence or short passage in turn, decide what the missing word or words might be, and send out a 'messenger' to examine the list. The 'messenger' reports back whether any of the words thought possible for that sentence are there, and if not what is, and the group completes the sentence or passage and passes on to the next one.

The game is a failure if the sentences are not hard enough.

## Variants

*A* The missing words could also be written separately on slips of paper, each word on more than one slip, and hidden, but not too thoroughly, about the room. If there is space enough and the class is small, groups find the words and make a note of them, then return to their seats and help each other to complete the sentences. If space is restricted, each group sends out a 'searcher' or two while it is studying the sentences. The 'search' should not take more than five minutes.

*B* Each learner writes a sentence on a slip of paper but leaves out one word, which should be fairly easy to guess. Each slip is then passed to the next learner, who fills in the missing word, writes another incomplete sentence, and passes it back to the first learner. The first learner corrects the attempt at completion if necessary, completes the second sentence, and adds an incomplete third. Now he passes the slip to the learner on the other side. And so on. Alternatively, the exchange can be with another team.

*C* As for B, except that the sentences are linked, each learner trying to add a sentence which seems to continue the story.

# 4 Dictation

Level **elementary, intermediate, and advanced**
Age **any (except young children)**
Group size **whole class, teams, groups**

Out of favour for a time, dictation is now seen both as a useful teaching technique and as a useful testing technique. Here we are concerned with learning and teaching. There are various ways of giving a dictation, and some will seem unusual enough to the learners to be regarded as games.

Probably the normal procedure is for a passage appropriate to the learners' interests and ability to be studied, possibly with the teacher's help, and then to be dictated as a whole. The learners do not see the text again until afterwards, when they correct their own mistakes or exchange papers and correct others', or do both. The number of mistakes is counted up and a score arrived at. 'Corrections' are done more or less at once, e.g. by writing out a number of times the phrase or sentence in which the mistake occurs. This is a game of sorts, although not a very interesting one, especially if the procedure is always the same.

## Variants

*A* The teacher reads a short and interesting passage aloud in a lively way, while the class follows it in print. Certain words and phrases which the teacher thinks need special attention are then written on the board while the learners study the text silently. The passage is dictated and written as a whole, and when the words and phrases on the board are reached the learners copy them. Some days later the passage is dictated again, fewer words and phrases being written up.

*B* The passage, or part of it, is re-worded somewhat when the dictation is given. For example, if it is a story the dictated text could retell it from the point of view of one of the characters. Or it could be dictated in another tense.

*C* The learners hear the passage, or a modified version of it, from a tape-recorder, with or without a text in front of them. They can then take it down from the tape phrase by phrase, the teacher using the 'temporary stop' button to enable them to do so. No phrase is repeated.

D  Where there are separate listening booths, learners can prepare the recorded passage at their own speed individually, with or without the help of a text.

E  A short passage is dictated, and then each group gets together and goes over it, agreeing on a version they believe to be correct. These versions are exchanged among the groups and checked against the text.

F  Dictate one side of a dialogue. This is then corrected and each group separately invents what the other speaker might have said. The teacher quickly checks these, correcting the worst mistakes, and each group leader reads them out to the class.

G  Groups prepare a short dictation, with the aid of the tape recorder and the teacher, and then each gives it (all taking part) in competition with the other groups.

## 5  Sentence relay

| | |
|---|---|
| Level | **intermediate and advanced** |
| Age | **children (except young children)** |
| Group size | **whole class, teams** |

There is the same text for each team, a series of sentences, arranged one on each line and all of the same length (very approximately). Preferably they should make up a brief story, or at least a continuous and interesting piece. Direct speech could be included.

The sheet is given to the first learner in each team. These learners study the first sentence and then either when they are ready or when the teacher says *Begin*, pass the sheet to the next member of the team, go to the blackboard, and clearly write the first sentence high up on their team's section of it. As soon as they are ready the next member of each team passes the sheet to the third member, and writes the second sentence under the first. And so on, until all the sentences have been written. If there are more sentences in the text than there are members of the teams (which should be equal in size) the first number takes over from the last and the writing continues.

Other things being equal, the first team to finish is the winner, but accuracy and legibility should be taken into account too.

Anybody failing to remember a sentence, or making a serious

137

mistake, must go back and study the sheet again, thus delaying the team effort.

## 6 Letter writing

Level **intermediate and advanced**
Age **any**
Group size **whole class, teams, groups, individuals**

Something of the atmosphere of a game can be given to letter writing if it is done in close co-operation with others and if the learners write to somebody real (e.g. for young children, Father Christmas; for older learners, an information bureau).

If parents are invited to a school play or concert, their own children should write the invitations. These will normally, of course, be in the mother tongue, but there is no reason why, coming from the foreign language class, they should not be in the foreign language too. The learners will feel this to be 'real' writing and will be encouraged if their parents are suitably impressed.

Letters to other classes or schools (perhaps also schools abroad) may be a joint effort, composed on the board with the teacher's help. Interclass letters in a foreign language are most easily arranged where two or more classes at about the same level are taught by the same teacher. Topics may include any activities in which the class or certain learners have been engaged, inside or outside the school, and any unusual things which have happened to any learners or in the neighbourhood.

If correspondence between school classes cannot be arranged, learners should write to each other. Unless the learners' grasp of the language is fairly advanced, it is advisable as a rule to have *some* oral preparation of such letters, and this will be welcome to the writers. There will thus need to be common ground in the subject matter, but this does not mean that everybody is discouraged from saying what she or he wants to say. It means, however, that there is a stock of common and well understood words and phrases to draw upon – a stock which can be added to in private consultation with the teacher: *How can I say (whatever it is)?*

Mistakes will be made in letter writing, but the main thing is that it should 'stretch' the learners' ability to use English by giving them an opportunity to communicate with somebody (in writing) something they want to communicate. They will not wish to make mistakes, and the teacher's help should be available, but to correct everything would almost certainly discourage most learners from attempting to make as much as possible of what they had acquired of the language.

In particular, correspondence with pen-friends, whether at home or abroad, ought not to be closely supervised or it will soon lose any excitement it has. Pen-friends should not be found too soon; be sure first that the learners can communicate, however crudely, something of what they want to say about their own lives and interests. Fairly advanced foreign language learners can usefully correspond, and can tell each other much of interest about the way they and their families live and about everyday life in their own countries. If personal friendships grow out of this exchange, that is something in its favour.

This applies to adult learners, except that they will doubtless like to be put in touch, using the foreign language as a lingua franca, with someone abroad sharing their own occupational or spare-time interests. Correspondence may also be possible on this basis with a native speaker of the language concerned[2].

# 7  Wall newspapers

Level  **intermediate and advanced**
Age  **any**
Group size  **whole class, teams, groups, individuals**

Here is yet another way of providing a motive for writing – to have what one has written 'published' for all to read. An editor and assistant editor are appointed, and perhaps reporters and correspondents and sub-editors of various sections: School News, Class News, Sports Page, Story Page, Joke Page, etc. Contributions can be added whenever they are forthcoming, so that the content is changing all the time. Although most items will be removed after a few days, they will be up long enough to make it essential to have no errors of language in them; the teacher therefore should assume the functions of an adviser and see that a fair copy of every contribution is displayed.

Different teams within the class can be responsible for different parts of the 'newspaper', but everybody should contribute something for it fairly often. If the class has enough language periods, it may be possible to set one aside now and then for the purpose of writing contributions. Spare-time writing ought also to be encouraged. The paper can be illustrated with line drawings; some learners love to add drawings to their written work.

Adult learners may also wish to contribute news items of current interest, readers' letters and arguments, notes on vocational themes, travel notes, etc.

# 8 Cartoon strips

| | |
|---|---|
| Level | **intermediate and advanced** |
| Age | **any** |
| Group size | **groups** |
| Time taken | **about 15–40 minutes, depending on the number of pictures in the strip** |

Some newspapers and magazines publish cartoons which tell a story. Choose those where no language is shown in the pictures themselves and cut away the language given underneath the pictures, which can be pasted on strips of card. The learners then study them and try to write suitable sentences underneath. This is difficult, and the teacher should try first to find out how difficult.

*NB*. Various tenses – e.g. present simple, present continuous, present perfect, past simple – can be used to tell most picture-stories. For instance: (1) *First, Mr Jones walks to the station and waits for a train. He gets in –* etc. (2) *What's Mr Jones doing here? He's walking to the station. And here, in the next picture? He's waiting for a train –* etc. (3) *Look, Mr Jones has left his house and is on the way to the station. Here he has reached the station and is waiting for a train –* etc. (4) *Yesterday Mr Jones left his house and walked to the station: you can see him here. When he got there he waited for a train –* etc. All these sequences and others could be based on the same picture-sequence.

## Variant

*Guessing the strip.* A different strip cartoon is given to each group (four or five people), but only one picture at a time, and out of sequence. The group discusses the picture, writes down one or two sentences about it, tries to guess something about the rest of the story, and writes down a little about that too. At intervals they are handed the rest of the pictures and each time they discuss them again, adding to and modifying what they have written. Finally, there is a written version of the whole story – in the synoptic present simple, or a mixture of the present continuous, the present perfect, and perhaps the future with *going to*.[3]

# 9 Consequences

| | |
|---|---|
| Level | **intermediate** |
| Age | **any** |
| Group size | **groups** |
| Use | **to practise past tense statements and direct speech** |

This is an old party game. Each player has a sheet of paper and a pencil and is asked to write down a man's name, fold the paper so that the name is hidden, and pass it on to the next player. The second step is to write *and* followed by a woman's name and to fold and pass on the paper again. Then come where they met, what he said, what she said, and finally *The consequence was that . . .*

Then the papers are unfolded and read out, with ludicrous results, such as *Charles Dickens met Snowwhite at Victoria Station. He said 'It's going to rain soon'. She said 'When's your birthday?' The consequence was that they both fell into the lake.*

Totally absurd, but many people love it.

## Variant

*A*   Each player writes *I* followed by *his or her name* and the words *resolve to* (= *make up my mind to*) on a piece of paper, folds it over, and passes the paper to the next member of the group. This player writes a New Year resolution (beginning with *to*), folds the words over again, and passes the paper on to a third, who adds *provided that* followed by someone else's name. Now the paper is folded and passed on once more, and a second resolution, introduced by *resolves to*, is added. The papers are then unfolded and the resolutions read out. For instance, *I, Rita Robinson, resolve to get up at six every morning provided that Sid Jones resolves to brush his hair more often* – and so on.

Just as absurd as *Consequences* but also entertaining.

*B* Everybody is given a different word or short phrase, and has to write the first sentence of a story, using and underlining this word or phrase. The sheet of paper is then passed to the next person, who writes a second sentence, but without using the word or phrase underlined. Then the paper is folded so that the first sentence cannot be seen, and is again passed on. The next person writes a third sentence, again folds the paper so that only this sentence is visible, and again passes the paper on. And so on until each sheet of paper reaches the person who wrote the first sentence on it. Without unfolding the paper, he or she then writes a final sentence using again the original word or phrase. The resulting comical stories are then read out.[4]

# 10  What would you do if ...

| | |
|---|---|
| Level | **intermediate and advanced** |
| Age | **children** |
| group size | **whole class, teams** |
| Use | **to practise conditional questions and answers** |

Team A writes down questions, each on a slip of paper, beginning *What would you do if* ... Examples: *What would you do if the roof fell in/you won £10,000/a lion entered the room/it began to rain very hard/you had no money to get home/the fire alarm rang/you lost your voice/there was a bus (railway) strike/somebody stole your bicycle/your car wouldn't start/there was no bread to be had/your TV set wouldn't work/the lunch interval was abolished*, etc.

Team B writes on slips of paper sentences beginning *I would* (but first give the class a normal example of the Team A and Team B elements put together), e.g. *What would you do if your bicycle was stolen? I would report the loss to the police. I would get under my desk/go for a long holiday/jump out of the window/put up my umbrella/walk home/eat cakes and biscuits instead/have it repaired/go home early*, etc.

All the questions are put into one bag or box and all the answers into another. They are all mixed up and then each player draws one slip from both receptacles and reads them out, e.g. *What would you do if you had no money to get home? I would put up my umbrella.*

The more questions and answers there are the more chance there is of a really funny sequence emerging.

### Variant

The questions can take the form *What would you have done if . . . ?* and the answers *I would have . . .*

## 11 True and false

| | |
|---|---|
| Level | **intermediate and advanced** |
| Age | **any (except young children)** |
| Group size | **whole class, teams, groups** |
| Use | **to practise reading comprehension and to contradict and correct false statements** |

See also Chapter 6.5, p. 103.

There are numerous general statements on the board, or statements based on a known story or piece of non-fiction. Examples of the former: *This school/college/institute is on the west side of town. There are no postal collections on Sundays. A TV licence costs more than . . . Dogs sleep in the daytime. In Britain the traffic goes on the left side of the road. There are more warm days in winter than in the summer.* Statements which are obviously true (or untrue) when made in the learner's native language need not be avoided; after all, one is not checking up on the learners' awareness of reality, but encouraging them in their efforts at using another way (i.e. another language) to talk about it. But for relatively advanced learners, there should be a number of statements which are not very obvious even in the first language – these will stimulate interest. Children, especially younger ones, like to be entertained now and then by the ludicrous, e.g. *Cats and dogs go to school. At the weekend the sun rises in the west. We put on our overcoats when we go swimming.* A variety of statements suited to the learners' ages is what is needed.

The sentences are read and then commented on in writing. There are several possibilities, all of which can be used, e.g.

True Yes, that's right, the college *is* on the west side of the town. (Also: that's true/that's quite true.)

True Yes, that's right/true/quite true, the college *is* on the west side, the traffic *does* go on the left side, etc.

False No, that isn't right/isn't true – That's nonsense/(quite) wrong/ untrue, the institute *isn't* on the west side, it's on the *east* side/there *are* collections on Sundays/there are more warm days in the *summer*/cats *don't* go to school/the sun rises in the east *every day*, etc.

Once the idea has been fully grasped, groups can invent and write similar statements and pass them to other groups, who will make written comments on them.

Points can be awarded.

# 12 Mini-novels

Level **intermediate and advanced**
Age **any (except young children)**
Group size **whole class**

The general lines of the story and main characters can be discussed orally first, or may be left to emerge gradually. Each learner writes, say, three sentences, and then hands it on to somebody else. From time to time a few minutes of a lesson period are devoted to reading out what has been written, and perhaps also to discussion of how the story should develop. This is an activity which should continue for a number of weeks. The story can become a little tortuous and unlikely – but never mind – the teacher will follow and guide it with good humour and probably with some surprise at the learners' powers of invention.

Such a story (mini-novel) could also appear, instalment after instalment, in a wall newspaper.

## 13 Broadcasting

Level **intermediate and advanced**
Age **any (except young children)**
Group size **whole class, teams**

Each team prepares a short 'radio programme' and this means a lot of writing. But instead of writing for the teacher's possibly weary eye alone, the learners write for the tape-recorder. This, with its microphone, is an imaginary radio station. All sorts of items, except very lengthy ones, are welcome – news, anecdotes, serials, songs (invented or real), fashion notes, interviews, business notes, notes on music and films, short debates and discussions, weather forecasts, accounts of visits, sports commentaries, etc., depending on the learners' ages and interests. Contributions are written first, then rehearsed and finally recorded. The recorded items are made up into a balanced programme and 'broadcast' to the class or school.

## 14 Write, read, and draw

Level **intermediate and advanced**
Age **any (except young children)**
Time taken **upwards of 15 minutes**
Group size **whole class, pairs, groups**

See Chapter 6.10, p. 109.

The instructions can be written instead of spoken. Instructions may be given to the whole class by means of flashcards. For Variants A and B, communication can take place by means of (legible) written messages. The teacher should move from pair to pair or group to group, smoothing out difficulties in response to requests for help, correcting misspelling, etc.

Those who receive the instructions may describe their finished drawings orally, and receive oral agreement or correction.

## 15 Builders[5]

| | |
|---|---|
| Level | **intermediate and advanced** |
| Age | **any** |
| Group size | **pairs, groups, whole class** |
| Use | **to practise giving and understanding exact instructions, and to stimulate talk** |

This is like the previous game except that, instead of a drawing, a construction is made – from coloured wooden bricks, meccano units, wire, plasticine, match-boxes – anything, in fact, from which a 'building' or structure can be erected. This construction can be made beforehand by one person or by a pair or small group, and must be kept out of sight of the others. But those who have made it prepare, as carefully as possible, complete step-by-step written instructions, which should enable anybody who follows them to reach the same result, given similar materials.

One problem here is to ensure that the groups have sufficient material to carry out their tasks.

If the same set of instructions is given to each group, the game can be competitive, the first to complete the construction correctly being the winner.

### Notes and references

1 See *The Teaching of English Abroad* by F. G. French, Part I, p. 80.
2 An up-to-date list of pen-friend agencies may be obtained (for English and other foreign languages) from the Central Bureau for Visits and Exchanges, Seymour Mews House, Seymour Mews, London W1H 9PE.
3 See 'Gulliver's Travels in Wonderland' by A. Maley in *Lingua e nuova didattica* 3, 17, 1976 for a similar game based on the cutting up of a single picture.
4 This variant is described by M. McGowan in 'That's how Uncle Walter's false teeth ended up in the marmalade': Two writing games, *Englisch* (Berlin), 2/78, pp. 57–8.
5 Adapted from *Communication Games* edited by D. Byrne, revised and amplified by S. Rixon, p.13.

# Chapter 9
# MIMING, ROLE-PLAY, AND 'LANGUAGE CLUB' GAMES

*Nearly all the games in this chapter take the learners away from their chairs and desks and give them a chance of moving about, as they do outside the classroom. First comes a group of games which involve miming, simulation, and role-play; then some games which are especially suitable for the voluntary 'Language Club' sessions that many schools organize, or possibly as spare time activities.*

## a) MIMING AND ROLE-PLAY

*Neither role-play nor simulation can be dealt with adequately in this book. Although obviously they should be mentioned, since they have about them the quality of games, they call for separate and detailed treatment. The same is true to some extent of miming, an element in a number of games already described. All these types of traditional activity are valuable aids to language learning and in some countries have for long been well established in primary and secondary schools. In recent years increasing attention has been paid to their use as a means of bringing more interest into the teaching of adults.*

*Role-playing is an aspect of simulation. A whole situation is simulated in the classroom, and the participants adopt roles which belong to it.*

*Children in general like any sort of play-acting, particularly if it means dressing up as the characters of a story. But they also like dramatizations of what they take to be 'real life', such as 'Doctors and Nurses', although what they say may not much resemble what is said in such situations by adults.*

*Role-playing (i.e. dramatization) helps to bring the language to life and to give the learners some experience of its use as a means of communication.*

*Much depends on the teacher's preparation, and on how well the teacher knows the kind of learner. What stories do they read and really like reading? What are the happenings of daily life which most thoroughly engage their interest? It may be that the children are delighted with The Three Bears, Red Riding Hood, Ali Baba, The Three Little Pigs, and such stories. The teacher should find out what appeals to them. But young children are also interested in the events of home – birthdays, feast days, visits to and from relatives, brothers and sisters, pets, and so on – and the teacher should be familiar with this background (foreground for the learners) if suitable subject matter is to be found for role-playing activities.*

*Older children, again generally speaking, are less interested in family doings than in what goes on in the wider world, and for many this includes adventure. They may also – but with numerous exceptions – have lost interest for the time being in the world of myths and gained interest in what they regard as the world of 'reality'; they are interested in clubs, gangs, and other forms of collective activity which adults tend to disapprove of or with which adults are not closely concerned.*

*Stories for dramatization should always be chosen with an eye to the roles they offer, preference being given to those which have several rather than two or three characters. The story must first be familiar, and then discussed from the viewpoint of what the characters in it do and say – or, rather, what they can do and say, for as much as possible should be left open for the learners' suggestions. Parts and passages of the action can be tried out with the whole class, somewhat in the manner of a rehearsal, and then it can be left to groups or teams to see what they can do among themselves.*

*There is now a large body of varied supplementary readers, at different levels of difficulty and suited to various age levels, which is one source of role-playing material. Accounts of personal experiences which the learners tell or write from time to time are another source. Maximum choice of roles should be permitted, but at the same time nobody should be inactive for long (hence the importance of groups).*

*Many adults will be learning the language for occupational purposes, and in some occupations it is used in fairly specific situations. In commerce, for instance, we have various salesmen-customer situations of planning and promotion in which various people have to confer. In medicine, for example, there are doctor-patient, doctor-patient's relative, and doctor-nurse situations.*[1]

*Role-playing for learners who require the language for vocational purposes ought to be based on an accurate assessment, which only those familiar with the vocation can make, of what exactly these requirements are. What is likely to need to be said and understood? How to explain, to request, to interrupt, to apologize – these and a score of other 'modes' of speaking may also be required.*

*'Acting out' the situations of the job presupposes some familiarity with the job itself, and the role-playing may in certain circumstances be a way of getting more familiar with it as well as with the language, the two being woven together.*

*One way of working is to start from the situation itself and to discuss what the various characters in it might say and how – the latter can also be important. It may well be that discussion of what should or might be said needs both to precede and to accompany the 'action' and that all participants should consider all the roles. After all, any conversation on any subject in any circumstances hangs together as a whole, and is not just separate utterances.*

*An alternative procedure – to be preferred if role-play is new to the class or if the class is not advanced in the language – makes use of role-cards, or cue-cards. See, for instance, 9.7, p. 156 below.[2]*

*The following games, in which the element of miming or role-play is prominent, have proved to be enjoyable and successful at different age and proficiency levels.*

# 1 What are they doing? What are you doing?

Level **elementary, intermediate, and advanced**
Age **any**
Group size **whole class, teams, groups, pairs**

Many simple actions which cannot be performed in the classroom can be shown in pictures or mimed, e.g. waking up, getting up, washing one's face, knitting, swimming, etc.

Learners and teams take turns to perform an action, and others guess what it is. After a correct guess has been made, the class or team can repeat it together.

Groups can separately prepare a number of mimed actions (not all the same) in which all the members of the group take part. Other groups then say what they think has been going on, e.g. an accident in the street (somebody walking suddenly stops, looks shocked, then hurries forward to help a man holding his head, is brushed aside by a 'doctor', etc.).

With advanced learners a broad range of mimed actions is possible, e.g. sitting behind someone big at the cinema, eating spaghetti/snails/tough meat/corn on the cob/an orange/grapefruit, etc. tying up/untying a parcel, repairing a fuse, trying to unlock a door with the wrong key, crossing a busy street, walking against a strong wind, wheeling a bicycle along a narrow path, walking along an icy path, trying to get a fly/wasp out of the room, sheltering from heavy rain under a small tree, etc.

It is also possible to mime *objects*, e.g. by using gestures to suggest size and shape and/or by miming the way they are used. Examples: a saw, an iron (for ironing clothes), a chair, a football, a tennis racket, a toy balloon (blow it up and pat it in the air), a microscope, a screwdriver, etc.

Although no language is involved in the mime itself, the mime stimulates interest, the desire to speak about what one has seen, and the wish to communicate to others that one understands what it represents.

## 2 Action chains

Level **elementary, intermediate, and advanced**
Age **any**
Group size **whole class, teams, groups**
Use **to practise one use of the simple present**

Action chains are linked series of actions belonging to the same broad situation, e.g. getting up in the morning (*I wash, dress, go downstairs, have breakfast, put on my coat,* etc.), arriving at school or at the office (*I get into the lift and go up to the fifth floor, I walk along a corridor, I enter Room 304 and hang up my coat, I sit down at my desk,* etc.) Adverbials such as *every morning, every day, often, on Saturdays, sometimes, at ten o'clock,* and at a more advanced stage clauses of frequency like *when(ever) I go by car,* are commonly associated with this use of the present simple tense.

Certain action chains can be mimed (as well as spoken) in the classroom, and the game is to get the items in the right order and to miss nothing out. While the learners are still only beginning to get familiar with this use of the present simple, there can well be certain chains which are more or less unvaried: the learners almost know them, and the actions that go with them by heart. A question such as *What do you do every morning?* or *What does X do when he/she gets home from school?* therefore, touches off a more or less set response of actions and words, and the other learners watch and listen to be sure the response is made fully. Members of the same team must not prompt one another.

Groups or teams may practise the chains separately before anybody does one in front of the whole class. Points are given for accuracy of language and action.

### Variant

The present simple is used similarly in demonstrations of how something is done or made in a series of steps. It may be a piece of cookery: *First, you take some flour and eggs and beat them together; then you pour . . .* (or, in the imperative, *First take . . .*). It may be the rules of a game: *Each captain chooses ten players, and the captains toss up to decide who shall begin. The one who wins the toss chooses from which end to play . . .* It may be a method of repairing something: *You get some glue and a brush and you put the glue on the broken edges . . .* and so on. If several learners can be found who know how to do a certain thing, it is best to let them work out an explanation jointly. It can then be discussed with the teacher and later put before the class as a competition item. If possible, objects and actions should accompany the talking.

It is wise at a certain stage to give the learners the vocabulary they need to explain how to do something they like doing and know how to do well.

## 3 The mulberry bush

This is a traditional singing and miming game which young children always enjoy. They join hands and run or dance round in a ring, singing:

> *Here we go round the mulberry bush,*
> *The mulberry bush, the mulberry bush.*
> *Here we go round the mulberry bush*
> *On a cold and frosty morning.*

Then they stand still and pretend to be washing their hands:

*This is the way we wash our hands,*
*Wash our hands, wash our hands.*
*This is the way we wash our hands*
*On a cold and frosty morning.*

Similarly: *This is the way we dry our hands/clap our hands/clean our teeth/brush our hair/clean our shoes/sweep the floor/run to school –* and any other suitable action. Individual children can sing the first line of each verse, or teams in turn can take the new lines while the others sing the refrain.

The tune is as follows:

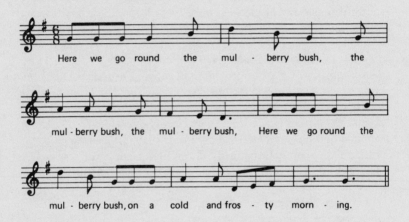

## 4 Round and round the village

This is a similar old action song. As the players, in a circle, sing the first verse, one dances round outside the circle. Next, they raise their arms to represent doors and the same player winds in and out round the circle as the second verse is sung. Then he or she stands in the middle and chooses a partner, by whom to be followed in and out of the circle again during the fourth verse. At the end, they both enter the circle and bow to one another. The partner then goes outside the ring and the song begins again.

*a) Miming and Role-Play*

1. *Go round and round the village,*
   *Go round and round the village,*
   *Go round and round the village*
   *As you have done before.*

2. *Go in and out of the houses* (3 times)
   *As you have done before.*

3. *Now stand and face your partner* (3 times)
   *And bow before you go.*

4. *Come follow me to London* (3 times)
   *As you have done before.*

Here is the tune:

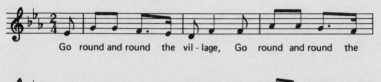

Go round and round the vil-lage, Go round and round the

vil-lage, Go round and round the vil-lage, As you have done be-fore.

## 5 Action songs

There are many such songs, several of which are suitable for the foreign language lesson. Here are some in English:

A.1 *One finger, one thumb, keep moving,*
    *One finger, one thumb, keep moving,*
    *One finger, one thumb, keep moving,*
    *We'll all be merry and bright.*
    (Finger and thumb held up.)

Then the words *one arm, one leg, stand up*, and *sit down* are successively added, all being accompanied by suitable actions.

2. *One finger, one thumb, one arm, one leg, keep moving*, etc.
   (Finger, thumb, and arm held up)

3. *One finger, one thumb, one arm, one leg, keep moving*, etc.
   (Finger, thumb, arm, and leg held up)

4. *One finger, one thumb, one arm, one leg, stand up, keep moving*, etc.
   (Ditto, followed by 'standing up')

5. *One finger, one thumb, one arm, one leg, stand up, sit down, keep moving*, etc.
   (Ditto, followed by 'sitting down')

The tune is as follows:

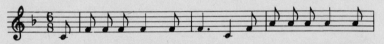

One fin-ger, one thumb keep mov-ing, One fin-ger, one thumb keep

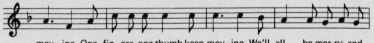

mov-ing One fin-ger, one thumb keep mov-ing, We'll all be mer-ry and

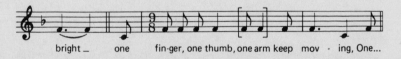

bright _ one fin-ger, one thumb, one arm keep mov - ing, One...

B. *Head, shoulders, knees and toes, knees and toes,*
   *Head, shoulders, knees and toes, knees and toes,*
   *And ears and eyes and mouth, chin, and nose,*
   *And head and shoulders, knees and toes, knees*
   *and toes.*

There is only one verse of this song, which is sung to the tune of 'There is a tavern in the town'. The singers touch the parts of the body mentioned.

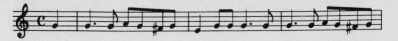

## 6 Charades

Level **advanced**
Age **any (except young children)**
Group size **groups**
Time taken **a whole lesson period**

These used to be popular with both adults and children, at Christmas and birthday parties, and were usually performed by small groups of three or four people. The group agreed on a word without telling anyone, then 'acted' each part or syllable of it, and finally 'acted' the word as a whole. Generally, but not always, the rest of the company was able at this stage to guess what word the group had chosen.

The 'acting' meant simply the introduction of the word once into a conversation, which might well be on some other topic. For example, if the word was *seasonable*, the word *sea* might occur in a short conversation among members of the group on holidays; a second 'scene' might introduce *son*, in a chat about somebody's family; the third part could be *able*, which might come into an exchange of views on how clever certain people are; finally, the whole word could be brought into a conversation on the weather.

If the words are to be hard to guess they have to be well hidden and this calls for ingenuity in the construction of the 'scenes', which may sometimes be almost on the scale of playlets. A fairly advanced group of learners is necessary, and also plenty of time. This is a type of game best suited to a school or other institution where the foreign or second language is also to a considerable extent the medium of instruction, and where there is enough time for such enjoyable language-using activities.

## Variant

Each group chooses a word, e.g. *coat*. Every member of the group then thinks of a word beginning with *c*, then one beginning with *o*, and so on. He or she then invents a mime to demonstrate what that word is. When everybody is ready, each group performs for the others, who try to guess the words represented by the mimes and from the initial letters discover the original word. Here is a possible sequence for *coat*:

1  C – cake, clean, carry, comb
2  O – open, offer, oil, old
3  A – apple, ask, ache, anger
4  T – turn, tie, twist, table[3]

# 7  Other people's shoes

| | |
|---|---|
| Level | **intermediate and advanced** |
| Age | **teenagers and adults** |
| Group size | **teams, groups** |
| Time taken | **half an hour or more** |
| Use | **to encourage spoken communication within specific situations** |

Role-playing can be supported by role-cards. One type of role-card states two interconnected roles, e.g. that of a manager who wants to appoint a secretary and that of a secretary applying for a job; that of a teacher who does not want to see a particular parent about her son, and that of a parent who wants to see the teacher.

There are many such cards, and they are in pairs: on one member of the pair one situation is mentioned first and on the other member the other situation, thus:

| | |
|---|---|
| *At school*  6<br><br>1) You are a teacher and very busy. At present you do not wish to see a mother who has called about her son.<br><br>2 You are a mother who has come to see your son's teacher to ask why he is given such difficult homework. | *At school*  6<br><br>1 You are a mother who has come to see your son's teacher to ask why he is given such difficult homework.<br><br>2) You are a teacher and very busy. At present you do not wish to see a mother who has called about her son. |

The game is best played by a small class or within teams. Each learner draws one card from the heap and studies it. Then he or she looks round for somebody who has a card bearing the same number, in this case 6. Then they make up a dialogue between them, one taking one part and one the other, and also alternating, and present this to the whole class or team, which guesses what it is about, asking questions if necessary.

Cards can also be used to define roles in a more complicated situation, e.g. a prolonged business conversation or a consultation among doctors and other specialists on how to arrest some epidemic.

# 8 Lost voices[4]

| | |
|---|---|
| Level | **intermediate and advanced** |
| Age | **any (except young children)** |
| Group size | **whole class, groups, pairs** |
| Use | **stimulates interest in asking questions (mainly 'yes-no') to solve a mystery** |

The basic idea is that somebody, having lost his voice, has to communicate with others by means of gestures. The others can be given a role, depending on ages and interests; for example, a teacher, a policeman, a hotel receptionist, a passer-by in the street, the information desk in a big store.

The teacher should have a number of slips of paper ready on which are written what those with the lost voices want to say. This should be very specific, e.g. (For a teacher) *I'm sorry I'm late but I overslept* (an easy one)./*I'm sorry I'm late but my bus went off the road at a corner and down a bank and finished up in the river – several people were hurt.*/*May I go home early today? My mother has gone into hospital and I have to get the tea for the other children.*/(For a policeman) *Come quickly, please, there's a burglar in our house, and he's tied up my mother and knocked my father unconscious.*/*My bicycle has been stolen. No, I didn't padlock it. It's an old green bicycle with no bell and two spokes missing in the front wheel.*/*My car has gone. I left it outside my house an hour ago – a red four-door saloon car. There were two suitcases in the boot and a small bag containing some bottles of wine on the driver's seat.*/*I've lost my dog – a large Great Dane, with its name on its collar.*/(For a hotel receptionist) *The telephone in my room doesn't work. It seems to be connected but I can't hear anything.*/*The dining-room is closed. Can I have two sandwiches and a jug of coffee sent to my room in ten minutes' time?*/*There's a fire on the floor below mine – smoke is coming through the floor, I think there's a child in bed there – quick, ring the fire brigade.*/(For a passer-by) *I'm looking for the zoo – which way should I go?*/(Fairly easy to mime) *Where is the nearest hotel and restaurant?*/(Another easy one) *This luggage is heavy, I want to get to the station by bus, not taxi*/(For the information desk in a store) *Is there a toy/furniture/sports/electrical department, etc. in this shop? If so, on which floor?*

A little time has to be allowed for the preparation of the mimes; otherwise they may be too crude and convey nothing. Then follows a kind of 'conversation' between the mimer and the rest of the class, who asks questions until somebody guesses what he or she is trying to convey. The mimer replies to suggestions by nods or shakes of the head, and perhaps grunts can be allowed too. It is important – for the sake of language-practice – that the full 'information' should be extracted; for instance, it would not be enough to establish that a car or bicycle had been stolen, without discovering what sort of car or bicycle it was and where it was stolen from.

Once this game has been played successfully with the class as a whole, it is better played in small groups or in pairs. Later, when the idea has been more fully grasped, learners will themselves contribute and write down 'situations' which can be passed from group to group.

Examples of questions and suggestions that might be put to somebody who had mimed the loss of a car (as above): *Was it a big/small car? Did you leave it outside a shop/in the car park/outside your house? Was it green/blue/black/red? Did it have two/four doors? Was there anything in the boot? A suitcase? Oh, two suitcases. Small or large? Did you leave anything inside? Where – on the back seat? On the front seat? What? Another suitcase? Oh, a bag. What was in it? Bottles? How many? Full or empty?* And so on. The answers are readily conveyed by gestures.

The more detail there is in the situation given on the slips of paper, consisting mainly of *yes-no* questions but to some extent of *wh-* questions, the more language practice there is for the class.

At the end of each episode what was written on the slip of paper should be read out.

# *b)* SPARE-TIME AND 'LANGUAGE CLUB' GAMES

*In many schools there is a voluntary spare-time 'Language Club' attended by students who particularly like learning languages and want to have some additional contact with the language of their choice. The 'club' meets regularly, sometimes in a special room, and there the learners have extra books and pictures to look at, more tapes and records to listen to and more games to play and songs to sing, not to mention more story-telling, puzzle solving, and other enjoyable activities.*

*Some of the games described in other chapters are also suitable for the 'Language Club' and for spare-time activities and special occasions, such as end-of-term parties for the foreign language class or birthday or name-day parties for those belonging to it.*

# 9 Matthew and Mark

| Level | **elementary** |
|---|---|
| Age | **young children** |
| Group size | **small groups, or groups of about 10 or 12** |

All but two join hands and form a ring. One of the two (Matthew) is blindfold and both are in the centre. Matthew calls *Mark, where are you? Here I am,* says Mark, but at once tiptoes away. Matthew has to catch Mark by listening to his voice, and so keeps asking *Mark, where are you?* Mark must answer every time, and cannot leave the ring. He may duck and dodge as much as he likes to avoid being touched by Matthew. When he is caught, Mark becomes Matthew and Matthew changes with somebody in the ring.

# 10 Blind man's buff

| Level | **elementary** |
|---|---|
| Age | **children** |
| Group size | **group of about 10–20** |
| Use | **simple questions and answers** |

A handkerchief or scarf is tied over somebody's eyes. This player tries to catch one of the others and guess who it is. *Who is it?* the teacher or other leader of the game demands. *It's Jack,* says the Blind Man. *Is it Jack?* the leader asks everybody. *No, it isn't* and the Blind Man has to let the captive go. If the response is *Yes,* the two change places and the captive becomes the Blind Man.

Alternatively, the teacher need not ask *Who is it?*; The Blind Man can just say *This is . . .* or ask *Are you . . .?* If the captive is wrongly named, he or she says nothing, but if the name is right, he or she must answer *Yes, it is* or *Yes, I am.*

Struggling out of the Blind Man's grip is not permitted.

The players should keep within a limited area, preferably rather small, and an unsuccessful Blind Man should not be allowed to continue too long: he or she should be given hints, e.g. the first letter of a captive's name.

## 11 Circle touch

Level **elementary**
Age **children**
Group size **small class, or groups of 12–15**
Use **to practise numbers**

All the players join hands in a circle. They number off in fours (or possibly in threes, fives, or sixes, according to the number taking part). The game leader calls out a number – for instance, 4 – and all the 4s run clockwise round the outside of the circle and back to their places, if possible without being touched by the 4 behind. When somebody succeeds in touching the runner in front, he or she calls out *Touch!* The one who has touched most players is the winner.

The numbers need not start at one; they could, for instance, start at 20.

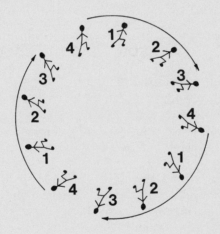

## 12 The moon is round

Level **intermediate**
Age **any**
Group size **group or whole class**

This is just one example of a whole group of trick games of this type.

Someone says *The moon is round* and draws a large moon on the blackboard. *The man in the moon has two eyes* – they are put in as amusingly as possible – *a nose* – drawn in similarly – *and a mouth* – and now the sketch is complete. (Alternatively, the man in the moon can be composed on the flannelboard, or even drawn 'in the air'.)

Other players must give a perfect imitation. But they will find it impossible to do so unless they have noticed that the performance begins with a cough, or with the performer touching his nose for a moment, or with some other irrelevant detail.

## 13 Have you seen my sheep?

Level **elementary**
Age **children**
Group size **whole class**
Use **to encourage careful listening and communication about dress**

A circle is formed, but one player, called IT, is outside it. He moves round the outside of the circle and taps somebody on the shoulder, asking *Have you seen my sheep* (or *dog*, *cat*, *goat*, *teddy bear*, or anything appropriate)? Reply: *What's it wearing?* or *How is it dressed?* IT then begins describing somebody in the circle, e.g. *A green pullover, black shoes* . . . (Or *In a green pullover* . . .). As soon as the one described recognizes himself, he runs round the outside of the circle away from IT. If caught before getting back to his place, he takes the place of IT.

# 14 Happy families

| | |
|---|---|
| Level | **elementary** |
| Age | **any** |
| Group size | **groups** |
| Use | **to practise simple requests and 'yes-no' questions; simple courtesy language: please, sorry, etc.** |

There are thirty-six cards, bearing pictures of nine families, each associated with an occupation. Thus there is Mr Cheese the Grocer, Mrs Cheese, Miss Cheese, Master Cheese; Mr Tape the Tailor, Mr Bones the Butcher, Mr Green the Greengrocer, Mr Fish the Fishmonger, etc. These cards are obtainable commercially or they can be home-made to suit the class.

The cards are dealt, face downwards, to everybody in the group. Each sorts his cards into as many families as possible and puts complete families face downwards on the table in front of him.

Players ask each other in turn for the cards they need to make their families complete, and a player must give up the card asked for if he has it. Thus the conversation goes something like this: *Can I have Mrs Bones, please? (No, I'm sorry, you can't). Please give me Miss Cheese (Yes, certainly, here you are). Have you Mr Bun the Baker? (No, I haven't, sorry)*, etc.

The one with the largest number of complete families at the end of a given time is the winner.

## Variant

A   Requests to other players could make use of conditionals, e.g. *If I give you Mr Green, will/can you give me Mrs Fish?* or *If I gave you Miss Bones, could/would you give me Mr Paper?* or *What could you give me if I gave you Miss Flowers?*

B   Each member of the class has one *Happy Families* card. If there are x families, x children come to the front of the class, each one representing a different family. In turn they ask individuals *What's your name, please. . .?* The reply refers to the character on the card held, e.g. *My name is Mrs Bones*, and if the questioner also comes from the Bones family, Mrs Bones goes out to join him or her, and puts the same question to somebody else in the class. If, however, the respondent belongs to another family, the next one in front has to ask. And so on, until all the families are complete. The first family to have all its members together in front is the winner.[5]

# 15 Beetle

Level **elementary and intermediate**
Age **any**
Group size **groups**
Use **to practise numbers up to six**

Each player has paper and pencil, takes a turn at throwing a dice, and can draw one part of the beetle (see below) if he throws a six. If he throws two sixes, he can draw two parts, e.g. two eyes or two legs, or an eye and one feeler. Whoever finishes a beetle first is the winner.

If you dislike beetles, try a spider, a butterfly, a cat, a monkey or a penguin – anything which can be drawn in a few definite lines.

Language comes into this game as the players call out the numbers thrown, and the parts of the creature as they draw them.

## 16 Obstacle race

Level **elementary and intermediate**
Age **children**
Group size **teams**
Use **to encourage accurate reading (verbs of action and prepositional phrases of place and movement)**

Example: *Walk along the white line, round the circle, and between the two buckets. Then jump over the stool and crawl under the rope. Run across the sand-pit and on the way back jump over the rope, run round the stool, and hop across the circle.* These are written instructions (containing a fine crop of prepositional phrases) and of course they need to be appropriate to the obstacle course which has been marked out on the playground or field. They also need to be longer.

The first team to have all its members back at the starting point is the winner.

## 17 Darts

Level **elementary**
Age **any (except young children)**
Group size **teams or groups**
Use **familiarization with spoken numbers**

Each group or team has a dart-board, like the one shown here, which is fastened on the wall at an appropriate height. The players in turn throw three darts at it, trying to hit the bull's eye (i.e. the centre of the circle). Those who do this score 50 points; otherwise only the number indicated. In order to have as much practice with spoken numbers as possible, each player should keep another player's score; this means adding it up with him – and he is sure to dispute it (and must do so in the foreign language)! Each team may have a score-keeper as well.

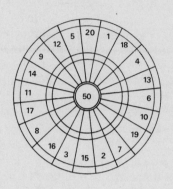

## Variant

Use a pencil with a blunt point. The 'dartboard' is drawn on a sheet of paper. Each player is blindfolded in turn and circles his pencil about over the 'board' before bringing it down decisively and as near the centre as he can manage, keeping it there until the scarf or handkerchief over his eyes is taken off.

# 18  Snakes and ladders

Level **elementary**
Age **any**
Group size **groups**
Time taken **half an hour or more**
Use **to practise spoken numbers**

*Snakes and Ladders* and similar board games provide incidental number practice in the foreign language, and children in particular get familiar with numbers in no time by playing such games. Small groups are best.

Each player throws a dice and moves his counter or button along a line, counting aloud.

In most board games of this type there are rewards and penalties. In *Snakes and Ladders*, for instance, whenever a player's throw brings him to a snake's head he is 'swallowed' and has to go back, whereas whenever it brings him to the foot of a ladder, he goes up it.

If games like this one are not available ready-made, they can be invented: simple and durable boards are easy to make with cardboard and linen, and once a specimen has been provided, learners can help each other to make their own.

## Variant[6]

There is a pile of cards for each group. In addition to shaking the dice each player takes one of these cards and asks somebody else in the group the question on it, e.g. *What was the weather like yesterday? What are you going to do this weekend?* These questions have to be answered by the player addressed. If they are sufficiently varied, and yet relevant to the learners' interests, a conversation can develop parallel to the number game.

Alternatively, requests and commands such as *Ask somebody what time it is. Ask your neighbour when her birthday is. Change places with somebody in the group,* etc. can be put on the cards.

It is also possible for what is printed on the cards to be closely linked with the game – *Move ahead four squares. Go back to the beginning. Your score is doubled*, etc. Or: *If you are on an even number, go forward to the next one. If you have been swallowed by a snake, miss the next snake*, etc.

## Notes and References

1 For a comical doctor-patient sketch, see 'Sketches and role-playing in your classroom' by J. N. Dixey in *Zielsprache Englisch*, 3, 1976.
2 For role-playing with cue-cards, see for instance, *Q-cards*, Paul Norbury Publications. For adult role-playing see *State your Case* and *English for Business* (business role-playing) and *English for Secretaries* (simulation).
3 With acknowledgements to Andrée E. Johnson, Teacher Training Institute, Nijmegen, Holland.
4 Adapted from 'The use of dramatic techniques in foreign-language learning' by A. Maley and A. Duff, in *ELT Documents* 77/1.
5 Adapted from *Faites Vos Jeux* by M. Buckby and D. Grant.

# Chapter 10
# DISCUSSION GAMES

*There are games in other parts of the book (for example,* Alibi *in* Chapter 1 *and* Other People's Shoes *in Chapter 9) which involve discussion. In this chapter, however, will be found a group of games in which discussion plays a dominant role. Most of these games lend themselves to group and pair activity.*

## 1 Who am I?

| | |
|---|---|
| Level | **intermediate and advanced** |
| Age | **any (except young children)** |
| Group size | **whole class** |
| Use | **to practise 'yes-no' questions and 'choice questions'.** |

Slips of paper are prepared beforehand on which the names of well-known people, e.g. pop stars, TV personalities, kings and queens of history, famous actors and actresses, popular characters in fiction, have been clearly printed. One of these is fixed by the party organizers to everybody's back, and nobody knows what the names might be.

Everybody then wanders round the room asking others *yes-no* questions, e.g. *Am I a man? Am I still alive today? Am I a pop-star? Do I live in America? Was I a king of England? Am I a character in a story?* As each player guesses the name on his back, he is allowed to move it to the front of his clothing.

Where people do not know one another well, this is a good ice-breaker.

### Variant

'Choice questions' e.g. *Am I a man or a woman?* are also allowed.

# 2 Find someone who ...

| | |
|---|---|
| Level | **elementary, intermediate, and advanced** |
| Age | **any (except young children)** |
| Group size | **whole class** |
| Use | **to find out information (questions and polite replies)** |

Everybody is given a list of people to find, for example:

*Find someone*

1. *who is exactly one month older than you are*
2. *who likes tea with lemon but doesn't like tea with milk*
3. *who has been to Britain without visiting London*
4. *whose birthday is on February 28th*
5. *who has less than* (a particular amount of money) *in his or her pocket*
6. *whose second name begins with G*
7. *who has a relative living in the USA*
8. *who has brownish-green eyes*
9. *who reads two Sunday newspapers*
10. *who gets up on weekdays before seven o'clock*
11. *who is a grandparent but has not yet retired*
12. *who lives more than ten kilometres from here*
13. *who is learning* (a certain language)
14. *who is going to be an air-hostess*
15. *who has two brothers and a sister*
16. *whose weight is less than . . . kilograms.*
17. *who will sing a song with you*

and so on. Whoever draws up the list should know who is likely to be at the party or meeting.

Armed with the list, everybody goes about asking others two questions at a time.

Example:

> *Excuse me, may I ask whether you were born in . . .?*

*Can you spare a moment? I'd like to ask whether you've ever been to Britain. Did you visit London?*

*Hullo, X. May I ask you an impolite question? Have you got more than ... in your pocket?*

Whenever the answer *yes* is obtained, the relevant item on the list is ticked and a note made against it of the respondent's name. After about ten minutes (with a list of 20 or more items) the mutual questioning ends and everybody adds up the number of ticks on his or her list. (The song should not be forgotten.)

There is a lot of conversation in this game and it is a good ice-breaker.

Terms of 'accosting': *Excuse me. Can you spare a moment? May I bother you? I wonder if you can help me,* etc.

Possible responses: *Delighted. Certainly. What would you like to know?,* etc.

'Negative' replies to a particular question: *Sorry, no. Sorry, I don't/Sorry, it doesn't,* etc. *I'm afraid I don't/haven't,* etc. *No, you've got the wrong person/you'll have to try somebody else,* etc. *But can YOU tell ME,* etc. (contrast stress).

# 3 Treasure island[1]

| | |
|---|---|
| Level | **advanced** |
| Age | **any (except young children)** |
| Group size | **pairs, small groups** |
| Use | **to practise how to find one's way** |

This is another kind of treasure hunt, based on maps. The searchers do not leave their places.

The location of the treasure is known – it is marked on the existing maps, which unfortunately are incomplete. You are at one end of the island, with one map, and your friend is at the other end, with another. How can you get to the treasure without being caught by cannibals, devoured by crocodiles, drowned in a swamp, swallowed up by quicksands, etc? Only by constructing a reliable map, so that safe routes can be followed.

Assume that your friend's map and yours together give all the information you need about the dangerous places on the island.[2]

You therefore need to consult one another in order to complete your maps and to decide how to reach the treasure. Fortunately you have two-way radios, so a conversation can take place. It might go like this:

A. *Hullo, B. Can you hear me?*
B. *Just. Speak louder, please. Where are you?*
A. *I'm at . . .*
B. *I can't hear.*
A. *I'm at . . . Where are you?*
B. *I'm at . . .*
A. *My map isn't very good – there's a lot missing.*
B. *Mine too. I don't know whether I can travel south from here – there's nothing marked.*
A. *According to my information, there's a tribe of cannibals just south of you.*
B. *Thank you for telling me. How can I miss them?*
A. *You're cut off by land. What about crossing the bay?*
B. *Too many sharks. I could probably get along the coast to the south-west.*
A. *Well, that looks all right, but it's a long way round.*

And so on. In the end they agree on two reasonably safe routes which will enable them to meet in the right part of the island.

This game, best played in pairs, could be prepared for (possibly a day or two before) by study of a similar map with the whole class. This could also be an incomplete map to begin with, and various hazards could be added as the problem of getting to a particular point is discussed. The learners would then be in a better position to play such a game in pairs.

If all the pairs have copies of the same two maps, a competition can be arranged, the winner being the first pair to solve the problem of safe routes. (The teacher should hold the solution in the form of a completed map with the possible routes indicated on them.)

## 4 Finding the way

Level **intermediate and advanced**
Age **any**
Group size **whole class, groups, pairs**
Use **to practise finding the way, routes, etc. using
'must', 'need', 'have to', and certain
prepositional phrases**

The basis of this game is a street map of a village, small town, or part of a city, either imaginary or real. There should clearly be marked the names of some of the streets and certain buildings or places, e.g. the railway station, the post office, the hospital, etc.

Two types of problem now present themselves for solution: (a) how to get from one place to another, (b) where you come to if you follow a particular route.

Here is the kind of language needed to talk about problem (a): *How do/can you get from the post office to the station? What's the best way of getting from the harbour to the Lion Hotel? Can you tell me the way to the hospital/school/shopping centre from your house? . . . First you go along* (or *must go along*) *Grove Road, then take the first (turning) on the left, go past the fire station, take the second on the right,* etc. *Go along Blossom Way until you see the church, but turn right before you get to the church, and then go straight on until you come to the Green Man, and then turn right,* etc.

But also language like this, if there is discussion of the route: *Need I/Must I,* etc. *go along Grove Road? No, you needn't go that way. You can go along the High Street and then . . . Yes, you must go along Grove Road, there's no other way of getting there, but you needn't take the first on the left, you can take the second on the left . . . No, you don't have to go that way, but it's the quickest way,* etc.

Problem (b) calls for language like this: *Start from the town hall, go along Richmond Road, turn left opposite the shops, take the second on the right – now where are you?* Or (an imaginary journey) *I'm at the library, I'm going to turn right, take the third on the left, cross the main road, turn right, and go under the railway bridge. What will I see in front of me?* Or *If you go along Oak Lane and cross the river and then,* etc. *where do you come to?*

If copies of the large map are mimeographed, so that each pupil has one, individuals and groups can make up problems for one another.

## Variants

*A* Such a game can be used as a means of acquainting the learners with certain aspects of everyday life in another country. The map could, for instance, be a map of the underground system in a major city, and on it could be marked not only the names of the stations but also of some of the places of historical or cultural significance nearby. Thus, using a map of London's underground: *What is there in Trafalgar Square? Nelson's Column* (Picture). *Who was Nelson? What else might you see if you went to Trafalgar Square at the weekend? A demonstration. How would you get to Trafalgar Square from . . . ? Where would you have to change?* Using a map of the Paris Metro: *How would you get to the Louvre from the Eiffel Tower? Is there more than one way?* etc.

Maps of a whole country or of the world can also be used.

*B* A map with sufficient detail in it can provide a useful basis for talk about the positions of various shops and other buildings: *Where's the chemist's/drugstore? It's opposite a jeweller's and next to a shoe shop. Can you find a bookshop? Yes, there's one on the corner of Broad Street and Lime Road.* Different groups and teams can draw up questions for one another.

Map-diagrams of amusement parks, zoos, university campuses, big stores, etc. – whatever is of interest to your class – may be used similarly.[3]

The advantage of using maps of the neighbourhood, or of some other place well known to the class, is that the pupils are more anxious to speak – to communicate their knowledge of where places are and of how and how not to get from one place to another.

*C* A place on the map can be indicated (not necessarily by the teacher) and two learners named as meeting there. These two are given a few minutes to go aside and invent a conversation – mentioning what they are doing, where (on the map) they want to go, and how to get there.

# 5 Telephone conversations

Level **upper intermediate and advanced**
Age **any (except young children)**
Group size **groups**

Two people, A and B, have a telephone conversation. We know
what one of them says (this is on the board or on mimeographed
sheets) and we have to guess what the other(s) say(s).
Examples

a Barbara *Hullo! Is that Mary?*
Sandra ............
Barbara *What time will she be in?*
Sandra ............
Barbara *Didn't she give you any idea?*
Sandra ............
Barbara *All right, I'll ring again after nine.*

b Jack ............
Tom *Yes, I'll call him. Jim! Someone for you on the
phone.*
Jack ............
Jim *Yes, it's me. What can I do for you?*
Jack ............
Jim *No, I couldn't get a ticket. What about you?*
Jack ............
Jim *Oh, thanks very much. How much do you want
for it?*
Jack ............

The conversations can be easy or difficult, short or long; they
may or may not be restricted to two or three speakers; and the
subject matter will vary according to the experience and interests
of the class.

Various possibilities can be discussed orally, or groups can be
asked to work out different versions and then 'act' them.

# 6 Likes and dislikes

| | |
|---|---|
| Level | **intermediate and advanced** |
| Age | **any (except young children)** |
| Group size | **whole class** |
| Use | **to focus the learners' attention on some point of spelling, pronunciation, or grammar, and to practise the third person singular of the present tense** |

See also Chapter 4.9, p. 82.

This is a puzzle as much as a game. It can be played as *I like* ____ *but I don't like* ____, or as *Tom (or somebody else) likes* ____ *but he doesn't like* ____, or perhaps as *Mr Nobody likes* ____ *but he doesn't like* ____. However we begin, others have to follow on in the same way, but it is not always easy to see what the same way is.

Let us suppose we are talking about Mr Nobody. The series of statements might go something like this.

| | |
|---|---|
| Leader | *Mr Nobody likes tea but he doesn't like coffee. Tom, please.* |
| Tom | *He likes milk but he doesn't like sugar.* |
| Leader | *Right. Mary.* |
| Mary | *He likes potatoes but he doesn't like carrots.* |
| Leader | *No. He doesn't like potatoes or carrots.* |
| Mary | *?!?* |
| Dick | *He likes lemonade but . . .* |
| Leader | *No, he doesn't like lemonade . . . Jane.* |
| Jane | *He likes juice but he doesn't like beer.* |
| Leader | *He likes juice and beer.* |
| Peter | *He likes cake but he doesn't like biscuits.* |
| Leader | *Right.* |

And so on, until it becomes plain that he likes things with names of one syllable and not two syllables. This is a comparatively easy one to solve.

Other examples:

A   likes cake but doesn't like biscuits.
       keys              locks.
       cabbage        potatoes.
       kebab           meat.
       (He likes things whose names begin with a /k/ sound.)

B   likes butter but doesn't like jam.
       hammers        nails.
       slippers         shoes.
       (She likes things with doubled letters in the spelling.)

C   likes soup but doesn't like soup spoons.
       water           jugs.
       cheese         olives.
       (He likes uncountables.)

D   likes beds but doesn't like mattresses.
       letters         the alphabet.
       tennis         rackets.
       pets           animals.
       eggs          ham.
       (He likes things containing the sound /e/ but not /æ/ in the first syllable.)

X   likes eating but doesn't like restaurants.
       heads         shoulders.
       dreams       sleep.
       the sea       waves.
       the ocean     ships.
       lead           tin.
       (He likes words containing *ea*.)

The verb need not be *likes*; it could be *eats*, *buys*, or something else, but this limits the choice of vocabulary.

The teacher (and it should be the teacher who leads this game) must have plenty of examples ready, although on any occasion there may be only a single type of example. This is primarily a spelling or pronunciation game, since the learner's attention is ultimately focused on a feature of spelling or pronunciation, but there is incidental familiarization with the -s ending of the third person present singular (*likes*), so often omitted by so many learners of English. It may be advisable to write the things Mr Nobody likes and dislikes on the board so that the puzzle can be easily solved.

# 7 Who is the baby?

Level **intermediate and advanced**
Age **any**
Group size **whole class**
Use **to describe people orally and in writing**

All the members of the class, including the teacher, bring photographs of themselves as babies, and these are mixed up before anybody has a chance to identify them. They are numbered and displayed, and the game is to guess who the babies are. Well-known people may be included too, if you can find their photographs in the newspapers.

One possibility is for the leader of the game to hold up the photographs (if they are big enough) one by one, and for the learners to make suggestions. *That looks like Mary – she has the same round face. That's Tom – he has a straight nose,* etc. (Owners of particular photographs keep quiet.) Another possibility is for everyone to write down their own guesses: *No. 1 is Mary,* etc. but this does not involve much use of language.

Probably the best procedure, if this is to be a 'language using' game, is to have some oral discussion about similar photographs beforehand, concentrating on such obvious points as the shape of the head and nose, the positions of the eyes, the hair, the size of the ears, etc. This can be quite interesting, especially where people like talking about one another. Among phrases which can be used are: *The ears stick out/are close to the head. The eyes are wide apart/close together. It has wavy/curly hair. It has a round/sad/lively/face. It has a long/big head,* etc.

After this preliminary discussion, using two or three other photographs, the learners are each given a sheet on which they can write something about the babies' photographs displayed on the walls of the room. So they move about, writing down such statements as *I think No. 5 is Linda because she has a short nose and a round face.*

More advanced learners will be expected to write more than the others.

It obviously helps if the photographs are in colour.

After everybody has finished, the guesses and descriptions are read out and discussed, and the solutions given. *Doesn't it look like me?* (the teacher). *How old were you when that photograph was taken, Bill? Alan has changed, hasn't he?* There is a lot of opportunity to talk, and usually a strong desire to do so, at least if the photographs are clear enough and the members of the class know one another quite well.

## Variant

The photographs are put in envelopes, which are mixed up. Each member of the class then takes *one* and writes something about it, including a guess. He or she then passes the envelope to a neighbour, who also studies the photograph and writes something else. Later, the descriptions and guesses are read out and discussed.

# 8 Which picture?

|  |  |
|---|---|
| Level | **intermediate and advanced** |
| Age | **any (depending on the pictures)** |
| Group size | **groups, pairs** |
| Use | **to practise following instructions** |

This game can be played in pairs or in small groups (say, of four people). Let us imagine it played between two on one side (A and B) and two on the other (C and D). Each pair has the same pictures, which may be simply drawn ones or more complicated printed ones.

The subject matter of the pictures needs to be suited to the learners' ages and interest. The general idea is that one side has to decide which picture the other pair is describing. This will be easy if the pictures are very different from one another. For instance, if there are four pictures to choose from – a beach scene, a street market scene, a picture of a rescue at sea, and a scene in a school playground – A and B will not get very far (e.g. *There are many people in this picture – they are buying and selling things*) before C and D have eliminated the last two, and they will soon narrow it down to the beach scene when A and B begin to talk about dress.

It is a different matter if the pictures are very like one another. Then they need to be looked at carefully, and there has to be exact use of language and attentive listening if successful communication about them is to take place. They can be pictures of houses with varying numbers of windows, doors, chimney-pots, etc. or roofs and curtains of different colours, or different kinds of trees and bushes nearby; or people with different kinds of clothing, hair-styles, facial expressions, etc.; or cars of different kinds and colours. Or they can be scenes (a village square, a station platform, a queue outside a shop, etc.) which resemble each other except for a few details.

A and B describe one of the four very similar (numbered) pictures, helping one another. C and D look at what they have in front of them and try to decide which picture is being described. After A and B have finished, C and D can ask *yes-no* questions on matters of doubt, e.g. *Did you say there are three people in the water? Are they swimming? Is one of them floating?* Finally, they give the number of the picture which has been described.

The 'sides' alternate in describing the pictures. For example, after A and B have communicated successfully with C and D about the beach scenes, C and D take one of the other sets, e.g. the school playground scenes, select one picture, and begin to talk to A and B.

If different pairs or small groups are given the same sets of mimeographed pictures, a team competition can be arranged, assuming that A (or A and B) in each pair (or group) belongs to the same team, while C (or C and D) in each pair (or group) belongs to the other team. A and B will in these circumstances not try to help C and D but C and D will ask follow-up questions as intelligently and quickly as possible (and A and B will have to answer truthfully) in order to identify the pictures described. The team whose members have accurately identified more pictures than the other team is the winner.

## Variants

*A*  One group of learners can see a picture and another cannot. Those in the second group ask *yes-no* questions (e.g. with a street accident scene, *Is there anybody on the ground? Is he taking notes?* etc. An occasional *wh-* question (e.g. *Where is the policeman standing?*) can be allowed in order to speed the process of 'building up' the picture. If there is sor ebody in the group or team who can draw well enough, the picture can be roughly sketched (and re-sketched) on the board as the questioning proceeds.

B   Two or three people build a structure of some sort with rods or sticks in full view of the rest of the group or class but out of view of the 'engineer' (who is behind a screen or a big box). Others then take turns in giving instructions to the 'engineer', who tries to build up an identical construction, also in full view of the class or the rest of the group. Gestures are not permitted.

C   *Artist.* One member of a pair draws on paper a simple picture containing matchstick figures, or a crazy cartoon, or perhaps an arrangement of lines and shapes (triangles, circles), e.g.

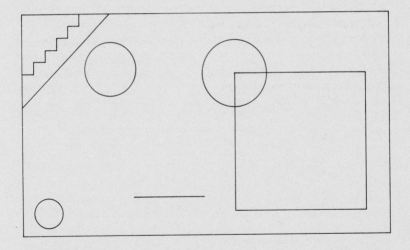

without allowing the other person to see. The two alternate in giving an instruction (e.g. *Draw a square on the left-hand side of your paper*) and asking a question (e.g. *Near the top?*). The first tries to be as exact as possible, in order to help the second.

A competitive game between pairs can be arranged if each pair has the same drawing.

*D   Picture Grids.* There are two people facing each other, but unable to see the other's grid of squares. In each square of A's grid there is a picture. B has the same picture but they are not on the squares. By means of questioning:

A:   *Put the bicycle in the top left-hand square.*
B:   *Right. What's underneath it?*
A:   *A car.*
B:   *Which car?*
A:   *The red one.*
B:   *Good. Where does the house go?*
A:   *In the third line from the bottom.*
B:   *How far along?*
A:   *Three squares along.*
B:   *From the left?*
A:   *No, from the right.*[4]

*E*   The class can see a picture but the teacher cannot. This is possible if there is a second board further back from the one on which the teacher has to draw, or if the class has mimeographed copies of pictures drawn by another person and not seen by the teacher. The 'game' is for the members of the class one at a time to tell the teacher what to draw. If anybody gives an inadequate instruction, somebody else must correct it. The teacher guides the instructing. For instance:

Peter:   *What shall I do next?*
Class:   *Draw a tree near the house.*
Teacher:   *Right. Which house, Jane?*
Jane:   *The middle one.*
Teacher:   *Right. On this side?*
Class:   *No.*
Teacher:   *Which side, then, Tom? etc.*

# 9 Looking out of the window

| | |
|---|---|
| Level | **intermediate** |
| Age | **any** |
| Group size | **whole class** |
| Use | **to practise 'yes-no' and 'wh-' questions** |

Somebody pretends to be looking out of the window, or really does look – what can sometimes be seen from the classroom window (a living picture) can be useful to the language lesson. He or she makes a bare statement, possibly no more interesting than *I can see a man*, which may be so or may not. The others, who cannot see out of the window, ask questions to fill the picture out, and the 'looker' must answer by supplying detail, either truthful or imaginary, e.g. *Is he old or young? Is he wearing a hat or coat? Is he walking or standing still? Is he tall? Is he talking to anybody? Who is he talking to?* and so on. Everybody should ask a question.

This is a game which should be played occasionally, as a useful time-filler. The questions can be extended to cover other people and things which can be observed or imagined.

# 10 One sentence each

| | |
|---|---|
| Level | **elementary, intermediate, and advanced** |
| Age | **any** |
| Group size | **whole class, and possibly groups** |

Somebody supplies the first sentence of a familiar story, and the others continue, one sentence each. The teacher's questions may be needed to bring out relevant detail – more than the bare bones of the story are required, except from elementary learners. The story should be long enough for everybody to have a turn or, alternatively, there should be more than one story.

## Variant

An unfamiliar story can also be told in this way, with more help from the teacher and from those who may remember parts of such a story. Or a new story can be made up, step by step, with the aid of discussion about the characters.

# 11 Advice column

Level **advanced**
Age **adults**
Group size **whole class, teams, groups**
Use **to practise giving advice**

Almost everybody is willing to offer advice, invited or·uninvited. Each learner is given one problem taken from the Advice to Readers columns of a popular weekly, and thinks out the advice he or she would give to the inquirer. A few minutes is allowed for this or it can be an overnight task. The same problem can be given to several people, who each explain and discuss their views with the whole class. The answer given by the journal itself is then read out and perhaps debated too.

## Variant

Instead of deciding upon their own advice, learners consult others living in the neighbourhood (especially those who speak the language they are learning) and report their views.

# 12 Cross-examination[5]

Level **intermediate and advanced**
Age **adults**
Group size **whole class**
Use **to practise various types of questions**

The teacher makes a statement, which might appear to be a casual one, and the class asks questions about it. For example: *I had a very good time last night. Oh, did you, where did you go? Who did you go with? What did you have to eat? Whose place did you go to? What was the play/film about?* and so on. What questions are asked will depend to some extent on the answers. Similarly, *I am going on holiday next week. Oh, are you, where are you going? Who are you going with? How long will you be away? Will you be going by plane or train?* etc. Various types of questions may be asked, including tag-questions (e.g. *You're going by train, aren't you?*) and 'statement questions' (e.g. *You're going alone?* or *I suppose you've booked the journey?*)

## Variant

This could also be done in groups, if various people have suitable statements ready.

## 13 Man from Mars

Level **intermediate and advanced**
Age **any (except young children)**
Group size **whole class, teams, groups**
Use **to revise known vocabulary and structures**

The basic idea is that one has not previously seen ordinary everyday objects and does not know what to do with them. So, for example:

A: *What's this?*
B: *It's a packet of tea.*
A: *Tea? What's that? What must I do with it?*
B: *Open the packet.*
(A opens it.) *And then?*
B: *You put it in a teapot.*
A: *A teapot? What's a teapot?*
(B draws or shows one.)
A: *You put it in a teapot. All of it?*
B: *No, not all of it. You need a spoon.*
A: *A spoon?*

And so on. An alternative title for the game might be 'Acting Stupid'.

Once the idea has been grasped, pairs of learners can prepare such dialogues themselves. They can be very entertaining. Possible topics: using tools of various kinds, what to do with a knife and fork, brush and comb, football/tennis racket/piece of string/radio set/camera/box of chocolates, etc. There is room for considerable ingenuity in the use of known words, and more words can be taught incidentally.

# 14 Who shall survive?

Level **intermediate and advanced**
Age **any (except young children)**
Group size **whole class, teams, groups**
Use **to practise conditional clauses**

This is an old game which takes a variety of forms. A number of people are stranded on a desert island and only some of them can be taken off in a small boat. Or a number of people are in a balloon which is rapidly descending towards a stormy sea: who is to jump out to enable the balloon to rise again, so that some of the occupants will survive?

The more specific the detail, so long as there is not too much of it, the more speech there is likely to be and the more interesting the discussion. The characters should be given occupations. There could be a doctor, a writer, a builder, a farmer, a teacher, a musician, etc. Whose work is most valuable? *If I am not saved*, says the doctor, *my patients will die*, while the farmer says: *If I cannot grow my crops, people will have nothing to eat*. And so on.

Each one makes a little speech – short or long, according to their ability in the language. Perhaps at the end a vote could be taken and people asked why they voted in a particular way, e.g. why nobody voted for the teacher.

## Variants

*A*  Instead of allotting roles and inviting those taking them to speak in their own defence, the characters and their occupations (and possibly their ages too) are given and then the problem is thrown open for general debate. Such a debate may be preceded by a period of silent preparation and making notes (and even perhaps by homework the night before) or by a period of informal oral discussion in groups.

*B*  Each of a limited number of characters is allotted to a group, which is given, say, ten minutes to prepare a defence, subsequently voiced by one member of the group in competition with representatives of other groups defending other characters. Each spokesman is expected to speak at some length and to be able to answer questions put by the rest of the class.

C   Each group decides on, say, the six or eight objects which would be most useful to someone, or to a group of people, stranded on a desert island. Each group chooses a spokesperson to explain and justify their choice and to answer questions asked by others.[6]

# 15   Silent film

Level   **intermediate and advanced**
Age   **any**
Group size   **whole class, teams**
Use   **to exchange information in the foreign language**

The class sees, at least twice, a short (ten-minute) film with action in it, but does not hear the sound, which has been turned off. Groups then discuss their interpretation of what they have seen: who are the people in the film, what has been happening? The film is then shown with the sound turned on. Subsequent discussion will make use of such language (in English) as *I thought they were . . . , I didn't think he was . . . , I was right/wrong in thinking that . . . , But it didn't look as if/he didn't seem to be . . .* , etc.

## Variant

Team A has seen the film with sound, Team B without. Team B questions A to get at the plot, etc.[7]

# 16   Conditional progress

Level   **intermediate and advanced**
Age   **teenagers and adults**
Group size   **groups**
Use   **to stimulate oral communication**

This contest could also be called *The Right to Continue* or *The If/Unless Game*.[8]
Each group needs a board or stiff flat sheet of paper on which a winding course or track has been marked out. This has a starting

point and a finishing point and consists of a series of squares or spaces in each of which a small picture has been stuck. These can be drawn pictures or cut-outs, and they should be clear and attractive. What pictures are used depends of course on the kind of class taught; they might be pictures of familiar everyday objects, of unfamiliar objects, of characters from stories read, of living creatures, of buildings, of vehicles, even of scenes and activities if the spaces are not too small; or of a mixture of such things. It is important that the pictures should look interesting.

For each group, there is a pack of cards and on every card a clearly printed 'instruction'. The players in turn draw a card, read aloud what they find on it, and have to justify any move forward to the others, who are free in their own interest to argue against it.

The 'instructions' are adaptable to the level of the class. They can be fairly simple, as in *If this is an animal that people can easily keep at home, move forward three squares* (e.g. a rabbit). *Unless you can buy this at any local supermarket, stay where you are; otherwise move on five places* (e.g. a box of chocolates). They can also be more difficult, as in *Go back to the beginning unless this is an object everybody needs* (e.g. a hat), or *If this wouldn't do much harm, go forward ten places* (e.g. a cigarette).

The 'instructions' should be of a kind to encourage argument. For instance, does everybody need a hat? An ingenious player might argue that, although many people do not wear hats, it would be better if they did, whereas the other players, anxious to find reasons for delaying their colleagues' progress, might argue that hats are unnecessary and that nobody need wear one. The teacher moves round the various groups, can join in the argument if consulted, and may have to act as an umpire.

## 17 Now you know

| | |
|---|---|
| Level | **intermediate and advanced** |
| Age | **teenagers and adults** |
| Group size | **pairs, groups, whole class** |
| Use | **to help people to get to know one another and to get them talking** |

This is a good 'ice-breaker' for a relatively advanced class the members of which do not know one another. If some members of the class are already acquainted, it would be better for them not to sit next to one another during this game.

First, the teacher (or a member of the class) introduces the game by saying: *I'm going to tell you something about myself. Look.* (Taking things from his or her pocket or bag) *This is a photograph of my husband – so now you know that I'm married. And this is my car key – so you know that I come to school by car . . . And what's this? It's a detective story – so now you know what I like reading . . . And this is a theatre ticket for last night – so what do you know now?* And so on.

The learners then show some or all of the things they have in their bags or pockets to the person sitting next to them, and ask one another questions arising from what is shown, e.g. *How long have you been married? What kind of car do you have? Who's the author? What was the play? Did you enjoy it?* etc. Conversation develops.

A further stage can be the introduction of one's neighbour to the class, using as reminders and focuses of interest the objects which have been shown. Others may also ask a few questions, and wider conversation may result.

This works best with a small class. If the class is a very big one, it is best to base the further stage on groups.

### Variant

There can be a middle stage, in which one writes down what one has learnt about one's neighbour. Some of these accounts can be read out to the class or a group, members of which may ask questions, e.g. *How long does it take her to get to school? How often does she go to the theatre?* and say things like *Ask her how far she lives from here* or *May I ask her what she likes to do at the weekend?*[9]

## 18 Doing one's job[10]

Level **intermediate and advanced**
Age **teenagers and adults**
Group size **groups or pairs**
Use **to practise some of the language needed in argument**

This is a game which calls for some ingenuity and imagination as well as a fairly good command of the foreign language. The basic idea is that one has a job and must justify the use of certain objects in doing it.

There are two sets of cards. Set A shows jobs or occupations, pictorially and/or in words: for instance, either a picture of a postman or the words *a postman* (or both). Set B shows various objects and animals, e.g. a bell, a telephone, a pair of scissors, a swim-suit, a hat, a ring, a ball, a chair, skis, a bicycle, gloves, a whistle, cows, a cat, a pipe, a dustbin, a comb, an aeroplane, a boat, a parachute – the more variety the better.

Each player takes a job card, and then each in turn draws one of the other cards from the pack and says how he or she would use it in doing that job. Questions can be asked and objections raised by the other player. For example, if a policeman says he needs a pipe to smoke when off duty, it can be pointed out that when he is off duty he is not doing his job.

Necessary language will include: *I need a/this ____ to ____. This ____ will be useful when ____. I can't think what use this would be. This would be of no use to me. I think I could use this ____ to ____. This would be essential when ____. I would use this ____ to ____.*

Each player keeps the card he has drawn if the others are satisfied with what he or she says; if not it must be returned to the pack.

The winner is the one who holds most cards after a certain time.

### Variant

The occupations may be symbolized rather than depicted. Thus, everybody would have first to decide what the symbol means. For instance, a book might be a symbol of a librarian or a bookseller, or even a student; a letter might stand for a postman or a stationer.

## 19 Eliminating the suspects[11]

| | |
|---|---|
| Level | **intermediate and advanced** |
| Age | **teenagers and adults** |
| Group sizes | **large groups or small classes** |
| Time taken | **15 minutes or more** |
| Use | **to stimulate the production of speech** |

This game bears some resemblance to *Alibi* (see p. 34), but there are many suspects, not simply two. For a group or class of 15, about 30 cards are needed, each of which bears a clear drawing of an adult or child who might have committed the crime in question. These people should have memorable features, such as a long red nose, a strange hat, a long beard, a funny hat, cross eyes, big ears, a weak chin, long eyelashes, or protuberant teeth, and in some instances their occupations should be evident from their clothes or belongings – a butcher, a clergyman, a postman, a teacher, a railway porter, a photographer, etc. The more striking and different they are, the easier they are to remember.

These cards are displayed in such a way that everybody can easily see them. They are given a few minutes in which to have a good look and to remember as many as possible. Then they are collected up and distributed, the same number for each learner, to all the members of the group; but one is held back secretly and placed face downwards on a table or fastened to the board. This card portrays the criminal.

Remembering the cards, each learner in turn says who committed the crime. Suppose the photographer is accused: the learner who has the picture of the photographer must defend him, perhaps by giving him a good character (saying what a lot of good he has done), perhaps by saying where he was and what he was doing at the time (establishing an alibi). Accusations and defences continue until somebody is mentioned for whom there is no defender: obviously this is the criminal, for whom a card is lying on the table.

## 20 Getting the full story

| | |
|---|---|
| Level | **intermediate and advanced** |
| Age | **teenagers and adults** |
| Group size | **whole class, groups** |
| Time taken | **15 minutes or more, according to the story** |
| Use | **to give practice in the use of questions to extract information wanted** |

One member of the group or class says *I've been reading a very interesting story*, but gives no detail except in response to questions, e.g. *Who are the characters? What are their names? Where do they live? How does the story begin?* etc. These will be general to begin with, but will inevitably become more specific, e.g. *Where did he get the gun? Did anyone see him on the way to the cave? How long did he stay there?* etc. The teacher need not know what the story is, and can join in the questioning, but the teacher's main role is to encourage variety in the questions. Provided that the story is a reasonably interesting one, and the class sufficiently advanced, conversation will soon develop.

Preliminary 'rehearsal' of the kinds of question that can be asked is necessary if the class is unfamiliar with this game. Such 'rehearsal' (using a very simple story as an example) should provide every learner with three or four kinds of question to ask.

It is an advantage if two people have read the story, so that one can help the other, especially if confusion sets in.

### Notes and references

1 With acknowledgements to R. Locke and R. Boardman.
2 The game can be complicated by having three or more friends at different places on the island, with three or more maps, incomplete in different ways.
3 See *Communication-Starters* by Judy Winn-Bell Olsen, Chapter 10, for some interesting ideas.
4 With acknowledgements to Judy Winn-Bell Olsen.
5 See *Teaching Oral English* by D. Byrne.
6 See *Buzz*, English Language Teaching Development Unit.
7 See Schumann J. H., 'Communicative Techniques for the Intermediate and Advanced ESL student' in *On TESOL 74*,

Selected papers from the eighth annual TESOL convention, page 232.

8 Slightly adapted from a game described by Shelagh Rixon, of the English Language Teaching Institute of the British Council, in her article 'The "Information Gap" and the "Opinion Gap" – Ensuring that Communication Games are Communicative', *ELT Journal*, XXXIII/1, October 1978.

9 This is a modified version of a game decribed by Roberta Vann in *English Teaching Forum*, XV, 4.

10 A slightly adapted version of 'Use It', described in *Communication Games*, edited by D. Byrne, revised by S. Rixon. English Language Teaching Institute, The British Council 1978.

11 Adapted from 'The Detective Game', in *Communication Games*, p. 68.

# SELECT
# BIBLIOGRAPHY

Aston, G. (1983) *Interact*. Modern English Publications.

Auge, H., M. Vielmas, and M.-F. Borot (1981) *Jeux pour parler, jeux pour créer: dynamique du groupe et prise de parole*. Paris: CLE International.

Berman, M. (1981) *Playing and Working with Words*. Pergamon.

Berman, M. (1981) *Playing with Words*. Pergamon.

Billows, F. L. (1961) *The Techniques of Language Learning*. Longman.

Bloom, J. and J. E. Blaich. (1970) *Lernspiele und Arbeitsmittel im Englischunterricht*. Cornelsen-Velhagen u. Klasing, Berlin.

Boucher, L. (1956) *Let's Play a Game*. Harrap.

Bruder, M. N. (1974) *Developing Communicative Competence in ESL*. University of Pittsburgh Press.

Buckby, M. and D. Grant. (1971) *Faites Vos Jeux*. Language Teaching Centre, University of York, for the Nuffield Foundation.

Burton, E. J. (1960) *Teaching English Through Self-Expression*. Evans.

Byrne, D. (1976) *Teaching Oral English*. Longman.

Byrne, D. (1978) *Materials for Language Teaching 1 and 2. Interaction Packages A and B*. Modern English Publications.

Byrne, D. and S. Rixon. (1982) *Communication Games* (second edition). National Foundation for Educational Research, for the British Council.

Caré, J. M. and F. Debyser. (1978) *Jeu, langage, et créativité*. Hachette, Paris.

Caré, J. M. and K. Talarico (1984) *Jeux et techniques d'expression pour la classe de conversation.* Paris: BELC.

Carrier, M. and The Centre for British Teachers. (1980) *Take 5.* Nelson-Harrap.

Chamberlin, A. and K. Stenberg. (1976) *Play and Practise.* John Murray.

Clark, R. and J. McDonough. (1982) *Imaginary Crimes.* Pergamon.

Cole, L. R. (1969) *Teaching French to Juniors.* University of London Press.

Crawshaw, B. E., C. Klauke, R. Klauke, B. Herbaux-Schmidt, H. Schmidt. (1985) *Jouez le jeu.* Ernst Klett, Stuttgart.

Crittenden, J. (1973) *Book of Fun and Games.* Mary Glasgow Publications.

Danesi, M. (1985) *A Guide to Puzzles and Games in Second Language Pedagogy.* The Ontario Institute for Studies in Education.

Derrick, J. (1966) *Teaching English to Immigrants.* Longman.

Dixey, J. N. (1976) 'Sketches and role-playing in your classroom', *Zielsprache Englisch* Number 3.

Dixey, J. and M. Rinvolucri. (1978) *Get Up and Do It.* Longman.

Dorry, G. N. (1966) *Games for Second Language Learning.* McGraw-Hill.

Dunlop, I. (1954) *Enjoy your English.* Stockholm: Folkuniversitets Förlag.

Dunlop, I. (1960) *Practical Techniques in the Teaching of Oral English.* Stockholm: Almquist and Wiksell.

Elton, C. S. (1966) *Allons Jouer.* University of London Press.

Finocchiaro, M. (1964) *Teaching Children Foreign Languages.* McGraw-Hill.

Finocchiaro, M. (1969) *Teaching English as a Second Language* (revised and enlarged). Harper and Row.

Fontier, G. and M. le Cunff. (1975) *Guide de l'Assistant de Français.* Longman.

195

French, F. G. (1948) *The Teaching of English Abroad*, Part 1. Oxford University Press.

Gibbs, G. I. (1974) *Handbook of Games and Simulation Exercises*. Spon.

Göbel, R. (1979) *Lernen mit Spielen*. Pädagogische Arbeitsstelle des Deutschen Volkhochschul-Verbandes, Frankfurt.

Granger, C. (1980, 1982) *Play Games with English*. Books 1 and 2. Heinemann Educational.

Greenall, S. (1984) *Language Games and Activities*. Hulton.

Gressmann, L. (1979) *Puzzles and Games*. Oldenbourg, München.

Hartmann, K. M. Schmidt, and H. Thomas (1967) *Darstellendes Spiel im Neusprachlichen Unterricht*. Munich: Manz Verlag.

Hassall, Peter John (1985) *English by magic: a resource book*. Oxford: Pergamon.

Hauptman, P. and J. Upshur. (1975) *Fun with English*. Collier Macmillan.

Hedges, S. (1973) *Games for Children while Travelling*. Ward Lock.

Hellyer-Jones, R. and P. Lampater. (1976) *Stories, Plays, and Games*. Stuttgart: Klett.

Herbert, D. and G. Sturtridge. (1983) *Simulations* (second edition). Nelson.

Hill, L. A. (1961) *Drills and Tests in English Sounds*. Longman.

Hill, L. A. and P. R. Popkin. (1969) *Crossword Puzzle Books*, 1–4. Oxford University Press.

Hill, L. A. and R. D. S. Fielden. (1974) *English Language Teaching Games for Adult Students*. Book 1: Elementary, Book 2: Advanced. Evans.

Holden, S. (ed.) (1977) *English for Specific Purposes*. Modern English Publications.

Holden, S. (ed.) (1978) *Visual Aids for Classroom Interaction*. Modern English Publications.

Johnson, K. ˚and K. Morrow (eds.) (1981) *Communication in the Classroom*. Longman.

Jones, C. (1975) *Structural Crossword Puzzles*. Longman.

Karnes, M. B. (1968) *Helping Young Children Develop Language Skills: a Book of Activities*. The Council for Exceptional Children, Arlington, Virginia.

Kerr, J. Y. K. (ed.) (1977) *Games, Simulations, and Role-Playing*. ELT Documents 77/1. The British Council: English Teaching Information Centre.

Kettering, J. C. (1975) *Developing Communicative Competence: Interaction Activities in English as a Second Language*. University of Pittsburgh Press.

Kleppin, Karin (1980) *Das Sprachlernspiel im Fremdsprachenunterricht: Untersuchungen zum Lehrer- und Lernerverhalten in Sprachlernspielen*. Tübingen: Gunter Narr Verlag.

Klippel, F. (1980) *Lernspiele im Englischunterricht*. Schöningh, Paderborn.

Klippel, F. (1985) *Keep Talking*. Cambridge University Press.

Klyhn, J. (1976) 'Hunting for Treasure in English', *Modern English Teacher* Volume 4, Number 3.

Koh, H. R. (1974) *Writing, Maths, and Games in the Open Classroom*. Methuen.

Krear, S. and B. Johnson. (1971) *Language Games and Songs for Core English*. Ginn.

Lee, W. R. (1960) *An English Intonation Reader*. Macmillan.

Lee, W. R. and M. Dodderidge. (1963) *Time for a Song*. Longman.

Lee, W. R. and Helen Coppen. (1968) *Simple Audio-Visual Aids to Foreign-Language Teaching*, 2nd edition. Oxford University Press.

Lee, W. R. (1970) *First Songs in English*. Oxford University Press.

Lee, W. R. (1973) *More Songs in English*. Oxford University Press.

Lee, W. R. (1970–73) *The Dolphin English Course*, I–IV. Oxford University Press.

Lee, W. R. and V. Maddock. (1982) *Getting Through Trinity College English*. Pergamon.

Lee, W. R. and B. Haycraft. (1982) *It Depends How You Say It*. Pergamon.

Lee, W. R. (1984) *A Study Dictionary of Social English*. Pergamon.

Livingstone, Carol. (1983) *Role Play in Language Learning*. Longman.

Löffler, R. (1979) *Spiele im Englischunterricht*, Urban und Schwarzenberg, München.

Lohfert, W. (1983) *Kommunikative Spiele für Deutsch als Fremdsprache: Spielpläne und Materialien für die Grundstufe*. München: Hueber.

Mackey, W. F. (1965) *Language Teaching Analysis*. Longman.

Maley, A. (1976) 'Gulliver's Travels in Wonderland', *Lingua e nuova didattica* Volume 3, Number 17.

Maley, A. and A. Duff. (1978) *Drama Techniques in Language Learning*. Cambridge University Press.

McCallum, G. P. (1980) *101 Word Games*. Oxford University Press.

McGrowan, M. (1978) 'That's how Uncle Walter's false teeth ended up in the marmalade: Two writing games', *Englisch* (Berlin) 2/78.

McRae, J. (1985) *Using Drama in the Classroom*. Pergamon.

Moretti, M. (1967) *A Book of Language-Teaching Games*. Milano: Trevisini.

Moorwood, H. (1973) 'Games based on solving problems', *Modern English Teacher* Volume 1, Number 1.

Moorwood, H. (1976) 'Scrabble – with variations', *Modern English Teacher* Volume 4, Number 2.

Mundschau, H. (1981) *Lernspiele für den neusprachlichen Unterricht*. Manz, München.

Olsen, J. E. Winn-Bell. (1977) *Communication-Starters and Other Activities for the ESL Classroom*. San Francisco: The Alemany Press.

Opie, I. and P. (1969) *Children's Games in Street and Playground.* Oxford University Press.

Paulston, C. B., D. Britton, B. Brunetti, and J. Hoover. (1975) *Developing Communicative Competence: Roleplays in English as a Second Language.* University of Pittsburgh Press.

Polívková, Dorota. (1963) *Hry pio jazykové vyučováni* (= Games for language teaching). State Pedagogical Publishing House, Prague.

Purkis, C. and C. Guerin. (1984) *English Language Games.* Macmillan.

Retter, C. and N. Valls. (1984) *Bonanza.* Longman.

Rinvolucri, M. (1984) *Grammar Games.* Cambridge University Press.

Rivers, W. M. (1968) *Teaching Foreign-Language Skills.* The University of Chicago Press.

Rivers, W. M. and M. Temperley. (1978) *A Practical Guide to the Teaching of English as a Second or Foreign Language.* Oxford University Press.

Rixon, Shelagh. (1981) *How to Use Games in Language Teaching.* Macmillan.

Root, Betty (1982) *40 Reading games to make and play.* London: Macmillan Education.

Rowlands, D. (ed.) (1972) *Group-work in Modern Languages.* Materials Development Unit, Language Teaching Centre, University of York.

Schmidt, E. (1970) *Let's Play Games in German.* Illinois: National Textbook Co.

Schmitt, U. (1981) *Buchstabensalat: 60 Lernspiele für Deutsch als Fremdsprache.* München: Verlag für Deutsch.

Schumann, J. H. (1974) 'Communicative Techniques for the Intermediate and Advanced ESL student', *On TESOL 74*, Teachers of English to Speakers of Other Languages.

Spenser, D. (1976) *Word Games in English.* Regents Publishing Co.

Thiagarajan, S. (1976) *Programmed Instruction for Literacy Workers.* International Institute for Adult Literacy Methods and Hulton Educational Publications, Chapters 7 and 9.

Trim, J. L. M. (1965) *English Prounciation Illustrated.* Illustrations by P. Kneebone. Cambridge University Press.

Via, R. and L. E. Smith. (1983) *Talk and Listen.* Pergamon.

Wagner, J. (1977) *Spielübungen u. Übungsspiele im Fremdsprachenunterricht.* Arbeitskreis Deutsch als Fremdsprache beim Deutschen Akademischen Austauschdienst.

Webster, M. and E. Castonon. (1980) *Crosstalk.* Oxford University Press.

Weiss, François (1983) *Jeux et activités communicatives dans la classe de langue.* Paris: Hachette.

Wright, A., M. Buckby, and D. Betteridge. (1984) *Games for Language Learning* (new edition). Cambridge University Press.

# PUBLISHED GAMES AND SIMULATIONS

Astrop, J. and D. Byrne. (1981) *Games for Pairwork*. Modern English Publications.

Brims, J. (1983) *Camden Level Crossing*. Pergamon.

Byrne, D. (1980) *A First Book of Board Games*. Modern English Publications.

Byrne, D. (1980) *A First Book of Board Games*. Modern English Publications.

Case, D. and K. Wilson. (1979) *Off-stage! Sketches from the English Teaching Theatre*. Heinemann.

Clark, R. and J. McDonough. (1982) *Imaginary Crimes: materials for simulation and role playing*. Pergamon.

*English for Business*. (new edition, 1985) Oxford University Press and the BBC.

*English for Secretaries*. (1978) Oxford University Press.

Hadfield, Jill. (1984) *Harrap's Communication Games*. Nelson-Harrap.

Hajnal, N. (1978) *Verb Bingo*. Longman.

Heyworth, F. (1978) *The Language of Discussion*: role play exercises for advanced students. Hodder and Stoughton.

Hicks, D., M. Pote, A. Esnol, D. Wright. (1979) *A Case for English*. Cambridge University Press.

Hines, Mary. (1980) *Skits in English*. Regents, New York.

Jones, L. (1983) *Eight Simulations*. Cambridge University Press.

Jones, K. (1982) *Simulations in Language Teaching*. Cambridge University Press.

Kerr, J. Y. K. (1979) *Picture Cue Cards*. Evans.

Lamb, M. (1982) *Factions and Fictions*. Pergamon.

Lynch, M. (1977) *It's Your Choice*. Edward Arnold.

Menné, Saxon (1977): *Q-cards*. Paul Norbury Publications Ltd.

Murray, H. (1973) *The big Deal*. Zurich: Hueber.

Niethammer-Stott, A. M. (1973) *Business Trip*. Zurich: Hueber.

Rixon, Shelagh. (1983) *Fun with English*. Macmillan.

Rogers, R. (1985) *Six Role Plays*. Blackwell.

*State Your Case*. (1976) Oxford University Press. Available from English Language Teaching Development Unit, 23 Market Square, Bicester, U.K.

*The Crisis Series*. (1974) English Language Teaching Development Unit, 23 Market Square, Bicester, U.K.

*The Case of Harkwood Ltd*. (1976) English Language Teaching Development Unit, 23 Market Square, Bicester, U.K.

Trim, J. and M. (1979) *Sounds Right?* Cambridge University Press.

Watcyn-Jones, P. (1978) *Act English*. Penguin.

Wakeman, A. (1974) *Jabberwocky*. Longman.

# INDEX

Game titles are shown in **italics**. Inverted commas are used to indicate words and phrases which occur prominently in games. Figures and letters in parentheses refer to the games and variants; figures in **bold type** refer to pages: thus **139**(8C) means 'page 139, game 8, variant C'.

**Games for:**

F
M
I
I